D1296131

DARK

PSYCHOLOGY

This Book Includes : "Dark Psychology for Beginners + Dark Psychology, Mind Control and Manipulation Secrets

By Michael Goleman

DARK PSYCHOLOGY FOR BEGINNERS

Table of Contents

Chapter 1: Introduction to Dark Psychology 15

    1.1 iPredator 17

    1.2 Cyber-stealth 19

    1.3 Arsonist 19

    1.4 Dark Psychology 24

    1.5 Dark Psychology Defined 25

Chapter 2: Manipulation Techniques and Tactics 38

    2.1 Effective Manipulation Theories 40

Chapter 3: Covert Persuasion 60

    3.1 Effectiveness of Covert Persuasion 64

    3.2 How does Covert Persuasion Work? 65

    3.3 Covert Persuasion Strategies 70

Chapter 4: Brainwashing 102

    4.1 What is Brainwashing? 103

    4.2 Brainwashing and Court Defense 121

    4.3 Brainwashing Techniques 125

Chapter 5: Effectively Analyzing And Influencing People 134

    5.1 Types of Influence 134

    5.2 Covert Influence to Trigger Impulse 138

    5.3 The Most Subtle of Subtle 143

    5.4 Secret of getting people to do a better job for you 146

Conclusion 147

References 154

DARK PSYCHOLOGY, MIND CONTROL AND MANIPULATION SECRETS

Chapter 1: Introduction To Dark Psychology Traits 160

Chapter 2: Vulnerabilities, Traits And Motivations Leading To Manipulation **176**

2.1 How Manipulators Control Their Victims *185*

2.2 Traits of People with Passive-Aggressive Behavior..........*205*

Chapter 3: Mind Control-Techniques.......................................**210**

Chapter 4: Covert Hypnosis...**236**

4.1 Techniques...*237*

4.2 What Hypnosis is and Hypnosis is not *245*

4.3 Covert hypnosis is a simple way to convince people *246*

4.4 Research-Based Evidence on Use and Utility *250*

4.5 The 3 Key Traits for a Hypnotist *259*

4.6 The Big 5 Hypnotic Power Words *270*

4.7 More on Covert Hypnosis Techniques *282*

Chapter 5: Brainwashing And Covert Persuasion..............**300**

5.1 Steps and Tricks for Brainwashing.................................*301*

5.2 Covert Persuasion Techniques.......................................*328*

Conclusion **345**

References..**352**

DARK PSYCHOLOGY FOR BEGINNERS

An effective guide to learn mind manipulation, covert persuasion, analyze and influence people effectively

By Michael Goleman

Chapter 1: Introduction to Dark Psychology

Humans have a built-in propensity towards kindness, empathy, benevolence, justice, patience, sincerity, contentment, courage, detachment, selflessness, generosity, honesty, conscientiousness, etc. However, humans, despite being bestowed by the said virtues, have to cope with other malevolent and devious traits that have been infused into their very being since creation. Humans are thus hybrid beings fully capable of doing morally appreciable and socially detestable and abhorrible acts at their own will. Humans who successfully manage to subdue their evil and deviant desires become paragons of excellence and morality in contrast to others who fall victim to socially unacceptable behaviors, impulses, and dispositions.

Dark Psychology is defined as the study of the human condition as it applies to people's psychological intent of preying on others. Humanity, as a whole, has this ability to victimize certain human beings & living creatures. While this urge is restrained or sublimated by many, others act upon these impulses. Dark Psychology seeks to understand the thoughts, feelings, and perceptions that lead to the behavior of humans relating to predators. Dark Psychology assumes this production is purposive, and 99.99 percent of the time has some rational, goal-oriented motivation. Under Dark Psychology, the remaining.01 percent is the brutal victimization of others without a purposeful intention or reasonably defined by evolutionary science or religious dogma.

"Dark Psychology is both the construction of human consciousness and the study of the human state, as it directly relates to the psychological nature of persons to prey on others, motivated by psychopathic, or psychopathological criminal drives that lack intent and general assumptions of instinctual drives, evolutionary biology, and theory of social sciences. All of humanity has the potential to victimize other living creatures and humans. While this urge is restrained or sublimated by many, others act upon these impulses. Dark Psychology investigates criminal, deviant, and cybercrime minds. "Michael Nuccitelli, Psy. D. 2006] Dark Psychology is one of today's world's most powerful forces at work. It is employed by the world's most potent influencers ever known—those who do not know about its risk it being used against them.

Some of the modern forms of Dark Psychology are:

1.1 iPredator

Within the next century, ipredators will become, if not squashed, a global phenomenon and societal epidemic with their acts of theft, violence, and abuse. iPredator divisions cover cyber-speakers, cyber-bullies, cyber-terrorists, cyber-criminals, online sexual predators, and cyber-war-engaged political / religious fanatics. Just as Dark Psychology considers all criminal/deviant behavior on a spectrum of seriousness and purposeful intent, iPredator's theory fits the same paradigm that includes violence, harassment, and online victimization using ICT. Any person, group, or nation that uses Information and Communications Technology [ICT] to exploit, victimize, coerce, stalk, theft, or dismiss others. The iPredators are motivated by deviant impulses, urges for power and control, revenge, religious fanaticism, political repression, psychiatric illness, perceptual distortions, peer recognition, or personal and financial benefit. iPredators may be of any age or gender and shall not be bound by economic status, race, religion or national heritage; iPredator is considered as a global concept used to identify those who use ICT to engage in violent, manipulative, deviant or abusive behaviors. Core to the concept is the idea that psychopathological classifications unique to humanity are the Information Age offenders, deviants, and the aggressively disturbed. Whether the perpetrator is a cyberstalker, cyber harasser, cybercriminal, online sexual predator, internet troll, cyber terrorist, cyberbully, consumer/distributor of online child pornography, or engaged in internet defamation or nefarious online manipulation, they fall within reach of iPredator. The following criteria are used to define an iPredator

- A self-awareness of harming others using ICT, directly or indirectly
- Using ICT to obtain, exchange and supply harmful information
- A general understanding of Cyberstealth used to participate in or profile illegal or deviant acts, classify, locate, stalk, and aim

Unlike predators before the Information Age, iPredators rely on the multitude of benefits that Information and Communications Technology[ICT] has to offer. Such help includes the exchange of information over long distances, the speed of transfer of information, and the seemingly unlimited access to available data. Intentionally malevolent, iPredators usually deceive others in the abstract and artificial electronic universe known as cyberspace, using ICT.

Therefore, since the internet provides anonymity to all ICT users, iPredators deliberately develop online profiles and diversionary strategies to stay undetected and untraceable if they want.

1.2 Cyber-stealth

It is an iPredator sub-tenet and a covert method by which iPredators strive to establish and maintain complete anonymity. At the same time, they engage in ICT activities planning their next assault, researching innovative surveillance technologies, or researching their next target's social profiles. Concurrent with the concept of cyber stealth is iPredator Victim Intuition[IVI], iPredator's IVI is their ability to sense ODDOR[Offline Distress Dictates Online Response], online & offline vulnerabilities, psychological weaknesses, technological limitations, increasing their success with minimal ramifications in a cyber-attack.

1.3 Arsonist

The Arsonist, is a person who is obsessed about setting the fire. These individuals often have a history of development filled with physical and sexual abuse. Common among serial arsonists are the tenderness to be loners, have few peers, and are fascinated by the setting of fire and fire. Serial arsonists are extremely ritualistic and tend to exhibit patterned behaviors regarding their fire-setting methodologies. Concerned with the setting of fires, Arsonists often fantasize & fix on how to plan episodes of their fire setting. Many arsonists experience sexual gratification once their target is set to ablaze and continue with masturbation as they watch. The serial arsonist draws pride from his actions, despite their pathological and ritualistic patterns.

Necrophilia Thanatophilia, necrophilia, and necrology all describe the same type of person being disordered. These are people who have a sexual attraction to corpses, and they do exist. The American Psychiatric Association's Diagnostic and Statistical Manual of Mental Disorders classifies necrophilia as a paraphilis. A paraphilia is a biomedical term. It is used to depict a person's sexual excitement and concern with situations, objects or individuals that are usually not part of normative stimulation and can cause a person's distress or serious issues. A paraphilia of a Necrophile is thus sexual arousal by an entity, a deceased human.

Experts who have compiled Necrophile profiles indicate that they have tremendous difficulty experiencing an ability to be intimate with others. Sexual intimacy with the deceased feels safe and secure to these men, rather than sexual intimacy with a living human being. Necrophiles, in the company of a corpse, has disclosed in interviews feeling a great sense of control. A sense of connection is secondary to the perceived power primarily required.

A serial killer is a true human murderer typically defined as someone who murders three or more people over 30 days or more. Interviews with most serial killers showed they are experiencing a time of cooling-off between each killing. The cooling-off phase of the serial killer is a mental refractory era, during which they are briefly satiated with their need to cause pain to others.

Experts in Criminal Psychology have hypothesized their motivation to kill is to pursue an experience of psychological gratification achieved only through brutality. After the assassination, these individuals feel a sense of liberation combined with selfish power. To them, the experience gives such joy that they become wanton to feel once again the feeling of independence and gratification.

"The term ' serial killings' generally means a series of three or even more killings, not less than one of which was committed within the United States, having common features." FBI rape, sexual assault, humiliation, and torture are often involved in their murders. Other motivations besides anger, rage, attention-seeking, thrill-seeking, and monetary gain, were outlined by experts at the Federal Bureau of Investigations. Serial killers often exhibit similar patterns in their choice of victims, how they assassinate their targets and body disposal methods. Criminal experts trained in conduct analysis agree that serial killers have a history of substantial behavioral, emotional and social pathology. Serial killers are usually loners who experience functional relationship difficulties.

Four examples of offenders and offender groups committing abusive and violent, bizarre acts that share the common bond of having profound psychological deficits with distorted worldviews are provided above. Those dangerous constructs of psychiatric or personality, which can metastasize throughout their being, defy reason. What about these human predators, how do they function in their everyday lives and socialize? These brief profiles speak volumes of the human condition's dark nature. Besides sharing mild to severe psychopathology, they are all perceptual loners with deep-seated forces that govern their decision-making capacity. As with the serial killer, the serial arsonist may not assault other people or find gratification from being a human predator. Still, from his setting on fire, he experiences joy and delight. This is a source of accomplishment for him. Additionally , he derives pleasure from the devastation that he has caused. His episodes of fire setting are dangerous, given that he can cause harm to others, but his modus operandi is not the goal of inflicting pain or bodily injury.

The big payoff for the serial arsonist is his sense of pride and distorted perception of bringing about a brilliant feat of genius. At times his perverted sense of accomplishment leads him to become sexually aroused, and masturbation follows. The conduct of the incendiary is reprehensible, illegal and dangerous.

They live inside an ocean of hellish madness. While the Necrophile does not cause pain to another human or victimize others, its acts are exceedingly bizarre and lack any sense of logic. The need for perceived control of the Necrophile is so insidious that it develops a sexual attraction towards a corpse. Imagine what it must be for him to feel. A lifeless body that is expressionless and devoid of blood makes him sexually aroused. Many people yearn for sexual intimacy, but this is not needed by the Necrophile. The experience of total and complete isolation makes him aroused—his mind shifts into a very dark realm.

One of the most despotic personalities manifesting from the dark side is the serial killer. The serial killer is often a subject of mystery in movies, court cases, and news coverage. The nature of this epitome of deviant horror echoes a part of the human mind, which can be felt only by the serial killer itself. The serial killer becomes addicted to murder just as an alcoholic person wants his next drink.

The serial killer speaks about the pleasure and elevated sense of freedom after his crime is over. Unlike the Necrophile or serial arsonist, the main goal of the serial killer is to quench life. They get sexually aroused by torturing their victims. Though a common theme, there are other equally disturbing drives that cause their victims to be tortured.

These four examples demonstrate the degree to which humans will go for the enjoyment of strength, gratification, and achievement of goals. All of the mentioned criminal profiles include attackers feeling gratified by their violent and heinous behavior. The fact is that these examples are merely simple portraits of four segments of the men and women's population that participate in violent, abusive, or deviant behavior. The degree to which humans are going to engage in sexual gratification, perceived power, or financial gain is quite extensive and complex.

Before the emergence of scientific advances and society's capacity to understand deviant human behavior, the origin of such confusion was ghosts and demons. Unable to understand how people could commit these crimes, the only logical explanation was supernatural entities. Primitive civilizations concocted legends and tales of demonic creatures instead of fearing their neighbors. Werewolves, Vampires, and Ghouls stalked their victims through the night.

While contemporary society considers itself as advanced in its ability to understand the human potential to commit violent and heinous acts, it remains elusive to learn how to minimize and prevent the human from bizarre and deadly behavior. We, the human beings, belong to the only group of living organisms involved in activities that are antithetical to our survival.

1.4 Dark Psychology

It is both the study of criminal & deviant behavior and a philosophical framework to discern the capacity for evil within all human beings.

It has been identified in the study of forensic and criminal psychology that aberrant, deviant behaviors are indicative of a psychiatric illness not yet established. With the passing of time and science, curiosity arose from the vast array of theories and reasons why humans possess an urge to prey on other human beings.

1.5 Dark Psychology Defined

Dark Psychology is defined as the study of the human condition as it has a relation to the psychological nature of persons to prey on other persons motivated by criminal and deviant drives, which lack intent and general assumptions of instinctual drives and theory of social science because life has that potential to harm other human beings and living creatures. At the same time, this urge is restrained or sublimated by many, some act upon these impulses.

Dark Psychology seeks to understand certain emotions, feelings, beliefs, and mechanisms of subjective thinking that contribute to aggressive actions that are antithetical to contemporary human behavioral understandings. Dark Psychology believes that violent, deviant, and abusive activities are purposive, and 99.99 percent of the time have some moral, goal-oriented motivation. It's the balance of the.01 percent, Dark Psychology parts from Adlerian philosophy, and Teleology. There is an area within the human psyche that Dark Psychology posits cause certain people to commit atrocious acts without intent. In this hypothesis, the Dark Singularity was coined.

Dark Psychology posits that all society has a reservoir of malevolent intent toward others ranging from minimally obtrusive and transient thoughts to pure psychopathic deviant behaviors without any coherent reasoning. This is called Dark Continuum. Mitigating factors that serve as accelerators or attractors to reach the Dark Singularity, and where the heinous actions of an individual fall upon the Dark Continuum, is what Dark Psychology calls Dark Factor. Below is a brief introduction to those definitions.

"Dark Psychology is not only our moon's dark side, but the dark side of all-stars combined." Michael Nuccitelli, Psy. D. Dark Psychology includes everything that makes us who we are in comparison to our dark side. This particular cancer is common to all cultures, all religions, and all humans. Throughout our life span, there is a side lurking all that some have called evil, and others have described as criminal, deviant, and pathological. Dark Psychology presents a third philosophical construct that takes a different view of these behaviors from religious dogmas and theories of contemporary social science. "It is the person who is not interested in his fellow men who has the most significant difficulties in life and who gives others the most severe injury. All human failures arise from among these individuals. "Alfred Adler Dark Psychology posits some people commit these same actions and do so, not for power, wealth, sex, revenge, or any other known intent. Without a target, they commit those horrid acts. Simplified, the goals don't justify its means. Many people, for the sake of doing so, abuse and injure others. The capacity lies within us all.

Dark Psychology believes it is incredibly complex and even more daunting to describe the dark potential. Dark Psychology believes that we all have the capacity for predator behaviors and that potential has access to our emotions, feelings, and beliefs. We all have this ability as you will read throughout this text, but only a few of us act upon them. For one time or another, we all had thoughts and feelings of having to act violently. We have all had felt that we want to hurt others without mercy severely. If you're frank with yourself, you'll have to admit that you've had thoughts and feelings that want to do evil things.

Given the fact that we consider ourselves to be a kind of benign race, one would like to think that these thoughts and feelings would not exist. Ironically, all of us have these feelings, and thankfully, never act upon them. Dark Psychology posits that some people have the same thoughts, feelings, and perceptions but act upon them in either deliberate or impulsive manner. The noticeable difference is that they act upon them, while others have only vague thoughts and feelings to do so. Dark Psychology claims that this type of predator is purposive and has some logical, purpose-oriented motivation. Religion, philosophy, psychology, and other dogmas have been forceful in their attempts to define Dark Psychology. It is true that most human behavior, linked to evil actions, is purposive and goal-oriented. Still, Dark Psychology suggests that there is an environment where purposeful behavior and purpose-oriented motivation tend to become nebulous. There is a spectrum in the victimization of Dark Psychology ranging from perceptions to total psychopathic deviance, with no apparent logic or intent. This continuum, Dark Continuum, allows the Dark Psychology theory to be conceptualized.

Dark Psychology discusses that part of the human psyche or universal human condition which makes predatory behavior and can even instigate it. Some of the features of this behavioral pattern are its lack of apparent moral purpose, its universality, and its lack of predictability in many cases. The universal human condition is believed by Dark Psychology to be unique or an extension of evolution. We have evolved from other animals, and that we are indeed the best of all animal life. Our frontal lobe allowed us to become the creature at the apex. Now let's assume that being apex creatures doesn't remove us from our animal instincts and predatory nature altogether.

If you believe in evolution, then you believe that all behavior relates to three primary instincts.
• Sex
• Aggression
• Instinct drive to self-sustaining is the three primary human drives

Evolution follows the survival principles of the fittest species and replication. We and all other forms of life function in such a way as to procreate and live. Aggression happens to mark our territory, protect our area, and ultimately win the right to procreate. It sounds rational, but in the purest sense, it no longer forms part of the human experience.

If you've ever watched a documentary on wildlife, you are bound to weep and feel sad for the antelope ripped to shreds by a lion's pride. The aim of the abuse, while brutal and tragic, matches the evolutionary paradigm of self-preservation. The lions are killing for food, which is necessary for survival. At times, male animals battle for the rite of territories or the will to conquer. All of these violent and brutal events demonstrate evolution.

The animals during hunting often stalk and kill the group's youngest, weakest or female. Although this fact sounds psychopathic, it is because of their chosen victims that their risk of injury or death is decreased. This way, all animal life acts and behaves. All of their brutal, violent, and bloody actions relate to evolutionary theory, natural selection, survival, and reproductive instinct. We humans are the ones in charge of what Dark

Psychology is trying to explore.

Once we look at the human condition, ideas of evolution, natural selection, and animal instincts, their theoretical tenets seem to disappear. We are the only beings on the face of the earth to prey one another for the species ' survival without justification for procreation. Human beings are the only creatures that prey upon others for inexplicable motivations. Dark Psychology investigates that part of the human psyche or universal human condition which allows predatory behavior and can even instigate it. Dark Psychology believes that there is something intrapsychic that drives and is anti-evolutionary to our behavior. We are the only species to murder each other for reasons other than life, food, property, or procreation.

Over the ages, thinkers and ecclesiastical authors have tried to explain the phenomenon.

Only we humans have a complete lack of apparent rational motivation to harm others. Dark Psychology believes that there is a part of which drives dark and violent behaviors.

This realm is universal within all of our beings. Today, before, or in the future, there is no group of people walking the face of the earth who don't hold this dark side. Dark Psychology claims that this aspect of the human condition lacks logic and meaning. It is a part of us all, and no definite cause remains.

Dark Psychology also assumes that this dark side is unpredictable. Unpredictable in the perception of who is behaving on these risky urges, and even more unpredictable in the lengths, some will go negated in their sense of justice. Many people rape, kill, torture, and assault without reason or purpose. Dark Psychology speaks to those actions of acting as a predator in search of human prey without clearly defined objectives. We are incredibly dangerous to ourselves as human beings and to every other living creature. There are many explanations for this, and Dark Psychology is trying to explore certain hazardous factors.

As described above, there was a multitude of philosophers, great thinkers, religious figures, and scientists who tried to conceptualize Dark Psychology convincingly. Dark Psychology encapsulates all previous theories and assumptions of violence against humans.

Dark Psychology occurs consistently throughout the human species and expresses itself without apparent moral motive as a predatory behavior (inclinations). Dark Psychology is like a spider's web trying to capture all of the personal victimization's previous theories and convey them to others that encourage empathy, and promote self-awareness.

The more you can imagine Dark Psychology, the more they are equipped to reduce their chances of being victimized. It is vital to have at least a minimal understanding of the Dark Psychology before proceeding further. Six tenets are then needed to fully understand Dark Psychology as follows: 1. Dark Psychology is a part of the human condition as a whole. This concept has had historical influence. Both cultures, communities, and the people who live within them uphold this facet of human health. They have this domain of bad, considered to be the most compassionate people, but never act upon it and have lesser rates of violent feelings and thoughts.

2.   Dark Psychology aims to explore the human condition as it relates to the ideas, sentiments, and perceptions of people associated with this innate potential to prey on others without clear definable reasons. Since all action is purposeful, goal-oriented, and conceptualized by modus operandi, Dark Psychology puts forth the notion that the closer a person comes to the "black hole" of pure evil, the less likely he/she is motivated.

3.   In its latent form, Dark Psychology may be overlooked due to its potential for misinterpretation as aberrant Psychopath. History is full of examples of this latent tendency to manifest itself as active, destructive behavior. Current psychiatry and psychology describe the psychopath as an unrepentant abuser for his practice. There is a spectrum of seriousness in Dark Psychology posits ranging from thoughts and feelings of aggression to extreme victimization and abuse without rational intent or motivation.

4.   On this spectrum, the Dark Psychology's severity is not considered less or more egregious by victimization actions but maps out a system of inhumanity. Comparing Ted Bundy and Jeffrey Dahmer would be a straightforward illustration. Both psychopaths were severe, and their acts were heinous. The difference is that Dahmer committed his atrocious assassinations for his insane need for companionship when Ted Bundy was murdered and

sadistically caused suffering from pure psychopathic madness. On the Dark Continuum, both would be higher, but one, Jeffrey Dahmer, can be better understood through his desperate psychotic need to be loved.

5.   Dark Psychology believes that all individuals hold the potential for violence. The ability is latent in all humans, and through internal and external influences increase the potential's probability of manifesting into unpredictable behaviors. Such habits are predatory, and can sometimes work with no excuse. Dark Psychology is simply a human phenomenon, and no other living creature experiences it. In other living organisms, aggression and mayhem can exist, but humankind is the only species that can do so without intent.

6.   A consciousness of the underlying causes and triggers of Dark Psychology will allow society to better identify, treat, and possibly reduce the dangers inherent in its impact. Knowing the principles of Dark Psychology serves a twofold function, which is advantageous. Second, realizing that we all have the potential to do evil will reduce the likelihood of it erupting by those with this knowledge. Understanding the tenets of Dark Psychology ties to our original evolutionary purpose of fighting for survival.

On the milder side of the Dark Continuum there is misuse of other people's property or the rising levels of violence in holiday season video games for children and adolescents. Vandalism and a child's desire to play violent video games is mild compared to overt violence, but they are clear indicators of this universal human characteristic. The vast majority of society condemns and covers their life, but the traits of Dark Psychology still lurk deeply beneath the surface in us all.

It's pervasive in society, and all over. Some religions describe it as a being they call satan. Most cultures believe that the culprits that cause malicious actions are the demons. Dark Psychology was defined by the brightest of many cultures as a mental condition, or spawned by genetic traits passed down from generation to generation.

We all have feelings, emotions and acts that, through cognitions and affective states, influence behavior. Conversely, a person's behavior influences his / her feelings and cognitions. Described as a network or what Adler called a constellation of the triad or trinity of human experience is composed as an interacting system of feelings, emotions and behaviours. Adler also contributed subjective interpretation to this paradigm of human experience. Childhood experiences, placement of birth order, family dynamics, consistency of social acceptance, and dynamics of inferiority vs. dominance function in a way that generates the persons' perception and course of engaging with his environment.

Visualizing a pair of sunglasses is the best way to understand emotional perception and the perceptual system. Such shaded glasses block out light and shield the eyes from harmful rays from the sun. Your eyes are a real reality, and the sunglasses are your filtering device that distorts the life of the harsh sunlight. Therefore, your "perceptual sunglasses" are filtering, distorting, and altering the way you perceive and respond to details.

The contextual reasoning functions like this but applied to the human condition. Reality exists and occurs all around us, every moment. Subjective thinking filters out our experience to shield us from what we believe may be counter-indicated to our purposeful objectives. If the person evolves in an environment where he perceives that he is part of, belongs to, and acknowledges, his subjective perception filtering system allows for more reliable feedback. When a person is socialized in what he perceives as a discouraging environment; his processing becomes distorted and convoluted with selfishness and narcissism.

Regarding Dark Psychology, the goal is to presume that all people use subjective thinking to filter their environment. Those hostiles, threatening, or abusive people wear a pair of proverbial, myopic, and fuzzy sunglasses. Such people perceive others as being out to hurt them and move first to threaten or exploit them. Their subjective interpretation distorts common decency, acts of kindness, and selflessness. Acts of kindness are impressions from abroad or used to exploit their social environment driven by an egoistic modus operandi.

Adler's postulated social value is the accumulation of experiences, emotions, and feelings that have been transformed into altruistic behaviors. Stated, the higher a person feels accepted by others, the more they feel a part of it, and the higher sense of belonging links directly to the social interest of a person. Inherently generous, selfless, charitable, and sensitive are people with high social importance. All of these Social Interest values further enhance their emotional thinking to be optimistic and compassionate. High Social Interest is equivalent to a low impact on Dark Psychology.

Because we all have a Dark Factor within us, his Dark Factor subdues the person with high social interest. The smaller the Social Interest, the higher the likelihood that the Dark Factor manifests. When a person feels disheartened, does not feel part of, does not experience a sense of acceptance, and perceives his environment as isolating, he is at a higher risk of unstable, violent reactions.

A section of the information relevant to understanding Dark Psychology is an outline that discusses the development of children, family dynamics, and other variables that serve to formalize Dark Psychology. While there is no way to accurately describe why and how certain people turn to the dark side, there are areas for research that help explain how the "laws of probability" occur in building the antisocial personality. Psychiatric disease, personality disorders, and alcohol/drug addiction as catalysts for deviant behavior are other areas explored. Mental and alcohol/substance abuse do not justify violent behavior, but these disruptions add to Dark Psychology's understanding.

Contemporary social sciences study the disorders of psychopathy, narcissism, and personality. Such profiles are fascinating in the world of forensic and criminal psychology and fuel much of interest.

This book aims to build awareness and understanding of the techniques of Dark Psychology and how to protect oneself from becoming a future human predator's victim. Once you have an understanding of Dark Psychology, then you will be able to assess the behavior of other individuals as potentially dangerous.

Dark Psychology is the science of mental control and manipulation. While Psychology is the study of human nature, and is fundamental to our feelings, behaviors, and experiences, the term Dark Psychology is the process through which people use techniques of motivation, persuasion, deception, and intimidation to get what they desire. It is the study of the human condition, as it applies to people's psychological propensity to prey on others. Humanity as a whole has this ability to victimize certain human beings & living creatures. Although many contain or sublimate this propensity, some act on these impulses

You can also apply the principles of dark psychology if you choose to. Please be warned, this book is not for the faint-hearted. You will have an understanding of human nature that few have ever obtained. With great power comes great responsibility.

Chapter 2: Manipulation Techniques and Tactics

Psychological manipulation is a type of social control that aims to change the behavior or perception of others through indirect, deceptive, or underhanded tactics. By advancing the manipulator's interests, often at the expense of others, these methods could be considered exploitative and devious.

Social influence does not always have a negative effect. Individuals like friends, relatives, and doctors, for example, may try to persuade people to alter obviously unhelpful attitudes and behaviors. In general, social control is viewed as innocuous if it respects the right of the affected individual to accept or reject it, and is not unduly intrusive. Social influence may constitute underhanded bribery, depending on the context and motives.

2.1 Effective Manipulation Theories

According to psychology professor George K. Simon, effective psychological manipulation mainly involves the manipulator with the following intent and actions:

- Hiding and being affable to hostile activities and behaviors
- Understanding the victim's psychological weaknesses to assess which tactics would probably be the most successful
- Having a sufficient level of ruthlessness to allow no misgivings about harming the victim if needed Consequently, the abuse is likely to be done through covert violent means.

According to Braike Harriet B. Braiker (2004), manipulators manipulate their victims in the following ways:

Positive Reinforcement
It includes encouragement, superficial charm, superficial compassion (crocodile tears), excessive apology, money, acceptance, gifts, publicity, facial expressions such as a forced smile.

Negative Reinforcement

It is practiced by removing one from a negative situation as a reward, e.g., "If you allow me to do this for you, you won't have to do your homework."

Intermittent/Partial Reinforcement

Partial or intermittent negative reinforcement may establish an efficient climate of fear and doubt. Partial or sporadic positive reinforcement may motivate the victim to continue–the gambler is likely to win now and again in most forms of gambling, for instance, but still, lose money overall.

Punishment

It involves nagging, shouting, silent treatment, bullying, threats, cursing, emotional blackmail, guilt trip, sulking, weeping, and the victim- playing.

Traumatic one-trial learning

The manipulator uses verbal abuse, explosive rage, or other intimidating actions to establish dominance or superiority; only one instance of such conduct can condition or train victims to prevent the manipulator from being offended, challenged, or contradicted. According to Simon, the following deceptive methods have been identified:

Lying (by commission)

It is hard to tell if someone lies at the moment they do it, although often the facts can later become evident when it is too late. One way to minimize the risk of being lied to is to realize that certain types of personality (particularly psychopaths) are experts in the art of lying and cheating.

Lying by omission

This usually is a subtle form of lying practiced by maintaining a substantial amount of the facts. They also use this strategy in propaganda.

Denial

Manipulator refuses to admit they did wrong.

Rationalization

An excuse for inappropriate behavior is made by the manipulator. Rationalization relates closely to spin.

Minimization

This is a kind of denial combined with rationalization. The manipulator argues that their behavior, for example, is not as cynical or insensitive as someone else suggests, saying that a taunt or threat was just a joke.

Selective Inattention or Selective Listening

Manipulator denies paying attention to anything that can detract from their goals, saying things like "I don't want to hear."

Diversion

The manipulator does not provide a direct answer to a straight question and instead is diversionary, moving the discussion to a different topic.

Evasion

It is similar to evasion, but with meaningless, rambling, and ambiguous responses.

Covert Intimidation

Manipulators, by using veiled (subtle, explicit, or implied) threats force the target into the defensive mode.

Guilt trip

It is an intimidation technique of a unique nature. To the conscientious victim, a manipulator suggests that they don't care enough, are too greedy, or have it easy. It usually leads the person to feel bad, leaving them in a position of self-doubt, anxiety, and submissiveness.

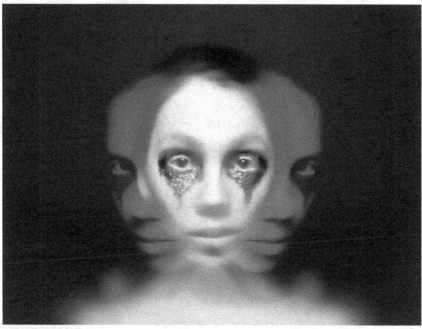

Shaming

Manipulator uses sarcasm and put-downs to heighten the victim's anxiety and self-doubt. Manipulators use this technique to make others feel undignified and unworthy by making use of shaming tactics, such as a stern look or smile, offensive tone of voice, sarcastic remarks, or overt sarcasm. Manipulators can cause one to feel ashamed even to question them. It is an effective way for the victim to build a sense of inadequacy. **Vilifying the victim**

This strategy is, more than any other, a powerful means of putting the victim on the defensive while still masking the manipulator's violent intent. In contrast, the manipulator falsely accuses the victim of being an abuser in retaliation when the victim stands up for or defends themselves or their role.

Playing the Role of the Victim:

The manipulator presents himself as a victim of circumstances or actions of someone else to gain pity, sympathy, or elicit affection and thus receive something from someone else. Caring and conscientious people can't stand to see someone suffering, and the manipulator always finds it easy to get help to capitalize on compassion.

Playing the Servant's Role: The manipulator conceals a self-serving agenda in the name of centered a more noble cause, for example, pretending that they are behaving in a certain way to be "obedient" to or "duty" to a figure of authority or "just doing their work."

Seduction

The manipulator uses charisma, encouragement, flattery, or openly supporting others to bring them down their defenses and give the manipulator their faith and allegiance. They will also offer help to gain trust and access to a charmed unsuspecting victim.

Projecting the Blame (Blaming Others) They manipulate scapegoats in ways that are often subtle and hard to detect. The manipulator will often transfer his thoughts onto the victim, making the victim look like they did something wrong.

Manipulators will also argue that the victim as if the victim induced the manipulator to be deceitful, is the one who is at fault for believing lies that they were conned into believing. The blame is done to make the victim feel guilty for making healthy choices, right reasoning, and positive habits, except for the portion that the manipulator uses to admit false guilt. It is often used as a way of manipulation and control over psychological and emotional matters. Manipulators lie about deception, only to remanipulate the less credible original story into a "more reasonable" fact the victim would believe. Another common method of control and coercion is to project lies as being the reality. Manipulators tend to falsely accuse the victim of being "deserved to be handled like that." They frequently say the victim is insane and violent, mainly when the evidence against the manipulator is present. Feigning innocence: Manipulator attempts to claim that any harm done was accidental or did not do something they were suspected of. Thus, the manipulator may put on a look of surprise or outrage. This strategy causes the victim to doubt his own decisions and probably his health.

Feigning Confusion

Manipulator attempts to play dumb by pretending that they don't know what the victim is talking about, or that they're puzzled about an important issue brought to their attention. The manipulator intentionally confuses the victim so that the victim questions their quality of perception, frequently pointing out key elements that the manipulator purposely included in the event there is room for doubt. Manipulators will sometimes have used cohorts in advance to help back up their story.

Brandishing Anger

The manipulator uses anger to brandish the force of frustration and indignation to scare the victim into submission. The manipulator isn't mad, and they just put on an act. They want what they want, and when rejected, they get "angry." Controlled rage is often used as a technique of deception to avoid confrontation, to avoid telling the truth, or to mask more aim. There are often threats the manipulator uses like going to the police, or to falsely disclose crimes that the manipulator deliberately created to threaten or bully the victim into compliance. Blackmail and other publicity threats are different types of controlled rage and coercion, especially where the victim rejects the manipulator's initial demands or suggestions. Anger is also used as a shield so that the manipulator can avoid telling lies at times or situations that are inconvenient. Anger is often used to fend off inquiries or suspicion. The victim becomes more focused on the rage, rather than the technique of coercion.

Bandwagon Effect

Manipulator allures the victim into submission by implying (whether true or false) that a lot of people have already done it, and the victim should do so too. These include phrases like "Most people like you..." or "Everyone does this anyways." Such coercion can be seen in cases of peer pressure, frequently happening in instances where the manipulator tries to manipulate the victim in trying drugs or other substances. **Effective Manipulation Techniques**

If you've ever fallen for a narcissist or a psychopath and spun your wheels combing through every image, interaction, email and text message searching for clues as to where things went wrong, what was real and what was false, and any indicators you may have overlooked along the way, what you'll come to find are the hidden traces of very manipulative and effective manipulation tactics used to seduce and control you. Pathological individuals (most commonly narcissists and psychopaths but also extremely manipulative non-pathological individuals) appear to be latent, master manipulators. And, when deception happens under the radar by its very definition and just outside the realm of our conscious awareness, it makes it very difficult to identify.

Manipulating people's emotions is much simpler than one might think. Consider what happened in 2012, for example, when researchers from two major universities teamed up with Facebook to perform an experiment in which they intentionally manipulated the feelings of over half a million Facebook users. For a week, Facebook updated a subset of its users ' newsfeeds so that half of them would see only positive stories and updates, and the other half would see only negative stories and updates. Once users in both groups posted their status updates as planned, they mirrored the mood of the posts and updates they had been exposed to.

What's troubling about this research is that if Facebook could influence its users ' emotions just by manipulating what they saw in their news feeds for a week, think about how easy it would be for someone to manipulate you, who knew you and had insight into what makes you tick?

Positive and Negative Manipulation

Essentially, we can classify the coercion techniques used by manipulative people to manipulate and control their victims into two main strategies: positive manipulation tactics for reinforcement and negative manipulation tactics for reinforcement. The term "positive manipulation tactics" may sound like an oxymoron since coercion is not considered a successful or a positive thing to do. Since that never is the case, though, the tactics are the most manipulative of all tactics.

Throughout the relationship, pathological individuals use both positive and negative tactics of reinforcement manipulation, but positive tactics of reinforcement are mostly concentrated during the initial phase of the relation. The narcissist or psychopath uses the prospect of some benefit or gain (positive reinforcement) to accomplish the following goals:

- Rapidly regain your confidence
- Lower your guard
- Win you over
- Invest yourself emotionally and often financially in the relationship
- Strengthen desirable habits
- Set up to take the abuse to obey

The following seven manipulation tactics are illustrated in the context of a romantic relationship, but they are used in all types of relationships. Not every narcissist and psychopath uses each of these

tactics, but many do so to some degree or another.
Charm

Isn't it ironic how that turns into the word harm when you delete letter c from the word charm? It's said you don't need anything else if you have charm. Writer Albert Camus describes charm as "The ability to get someone to say" yes "without posing a clear question." Charm is usually the first hint that you may be in a manipulative person's crosshairs.

Narcissists and psychopaths after one encounter will leave you feeling like you've known them for years. They can be smooth, friendly, warm, confident, and they always seem to know exactly what to say. Even though, if you stick around them long enough, you'll probably notice that those witty comebacks are just a bunch of rehearsed lines that they recycle with every new person they meet. Narcissists and psychopaths use the charm techniques to establish a connection with you quickly, so you'll lower your guard immediately and not be tipped off to their selfserving agendas.

Society forces us to perceive beauty as an appealing and positive attribute but, according to the author, Lundy Bancroft, "People who choose to put that much excessive effort into the way they present themselves often do so because they have something to hide. We move around the world, taking advantage of people, so in a package that looks appealing or everyone would run away from them, we need to put their way of operating. Usually, the exploiters are charming."
Me Too!

Part of the charm of the addictive personality is the willingness to let you feel like you both are amazing, and so much the same. We're drawn to people who share common interests, ambitions, preferences, beliefs and understand us at a level many people don't. You know the instant bond feeling you get when you meet someone and reveal something about yourself, and they're answering with, "Me too! "Not only do these two little words express empathy, understanding, and the assurance of I get you, but they can also be profoundly bonding.

We expect a more favorable opinion immediately and are quicker to trust people who remind us of ourselves, which is why narcissists and psychopaths claim to have the same beliefs and views as their goals. Their uncanny ability to convincingly morph into your perfect match is why it's so hard to believe when we see them change their whole identities and going from being someone who was a hardcore red meat-eating, country music-loving, traditional, foodie to unexpectedly pretending to be a bohemian, alternative music-loving vegan in the next relationship.

Furthermore, by using a tactic called mirroring, establishing relationships and bonding by "similarity" can be communicated just as actively, if not more so, in non-verbal ways. Mirroring is a proactive listening strategy that not only represents the substance of the disclosure of the client but also closely emulates other features of their non-verbal behavior, such as; the sound and pace of their voice, their mannerisms, and the language of their body. Simply put, mirroring is a useful tool to connect with people and influence their feelings. It is because we all have cells in our brains called mirror neurons. These mirror neurons respond the same way, whether we are performing an action (that is, throwing a ball) or observing an effort (that is, watching someone throw a ball). So, when our actions are unconsciously reflected on us, the reciprocal firing of our mirror neurons strengthens our partnership feelings and generates similarity perception. When salespeople were instructed to use mirroring techniques with their customers, numerous studies confirmed their customers responded more approvingly, and they gave higher ratings on customer satisfaction surveys. **The Illusion of Intimacy**

The faster the narcissist or psychopath can get you emotionally and financially invested in them, the less time they have to spend keeping up with Mr./Ms. Nice guy/gal act, and can begin by manipulating and controlling you to concentrate on their real goalmeeting their needs. Upon meeting you, the narcissist or psychopath will deliberately share something very intimate with you to achieve the illusion of intimacy quickly and gain your confidence. However, they will share it in a way that makes them look genuine and insecure, not socially awkward, as in the manner of a TMI (Too Much Information). Another way for narcissists and psychopaths to use the illusion of intimacy is to suggest that there are higher powers or forces involved in bringing together the two of you. It might be Allah, the cosmos, the stars, the supernatural, destiny, or anything that could appeal to your spiritual side. And who are you to doubt the divine will, after all?

Love Bombing

You know you're bombed when the constant displays of affection and adoration make you feel dizzy. This is a common tactic for lowering your defenses, knocking off your balance, and getting you to commit quickly, but it also plays a part in keeping you hooked. All that self-esteem boosting attention, adoration, and flattery also provide short-term, dopamine-level boosting. The neurotransmitter dopamine gives you that small rush of pleasure and energy when you're bombarded with love. Over time, the brain starts associating the love bomber with the pleasure-inducing chemical dopamine spikes. So, when the bombing of love stops and the violence begins, it can feel like withdrawal of drugs and send you into frenzy-seeking dopamine.

Social media and smartphones are a favorite tool for love bomber as they allow greater access to the target and the means for constant communication and more intense love bombing. A narcissist could blow up your social media with comments, likes, Snapchat, tweets, and DM's. They could be sending you around the clock. "I'm just thinking about you," tell text messages and kissy-face emojis, or call you and talk to you on the phone for hours. They will shower you with expressions of everlasting, lasting love, declarations of soul mate status very early on in the relationship, or send you gifts or tokens of affection. Among the many hard things on of the hardest thing to avoid is love bombing from someone you're interested in and attracted to because it not only appeals to your natural desire to feel loved and appreciated, but it will cause you to ask yourself, "How can something that feels so good be wrong?"

Carrot Dangling

Carrot dangling happens once the narcissist or psychopath has determined what you want and has taken stock of your future dreams (i.e., love, friendship, marriage, babies, holidays in Italy, country house, and so on...) which will, of course, suit their desires and future dreams together. Not only will they reassure you that they share your goals and vision for the future, but they will also be able and will make them come true. But, since they have no intention of satisfying your wishes and potential hopes, they will lead you on by always hanging in front of you glimpses of hope and promises of a future together (future faking), but only slightly out of control.

Trance

Pathologic people use trance and hypnosis to seduce and manipulate their targets, which is a relaxed state of high suggestibility. They manipulate their subject into a trance state by using a variety of strategies that can include; a rhythmic tone of voice, strength, repeated eye-contact and repetition, and then verbally plant suggestions into their subconscious mind.

The subconscious mind, unlike the conscious mind, does not use logic, reason, or even think for itself. Its purpose is to store data permanently and to follow commands. The knowledge that gets placed in your subconscious mind remains there forever and causes you to act accordingly.

Research studies have also shown that just the act of gazing warmly, non-aggressively into someone's eyes for ten minutes or longer creates altered states of consciousness. Mostly, look lovingly into the eyes of your lover for an extended period and say things like, "Do you see your future? "We are perfect together" is not only perceived as intense, romantic, and bonding, but it can be a powerful form of mind control.

Isolation

The isolation technique is used to accomplish three main goals. To detach you from your loved ones ' guidance and power To preemptively reduce your circle of social support so that you won't have others to turn to once the violence starts to cause you to be reliant on and focus solely on the narcissist or psychopath This strategy will probably fit into both categories depending on how it is performed. Nonetheless, while the loss of social support is an adverse effect of isolation, it is not exploited through explicit or implicit threats of failure, retribution, rejection, or abandonment, but it could certainly be. Additionally, a significant amount of time spent with the pathological person during the initial phase of the relationship is usually desired by the client and viewed as enjoyable.

The technique of solitude can be easily missed early in the relationship because it is common to yearn to spend maximum time with a new loved one. The manipulator might say things like, "I want to spend all my free time with you as I am in love with you." Or they might take something you've said about a trustworthy friend and use it to their advantage. For instance, "I don't like you hanging out with Judy because I'm worried that she'll stab you as she did with your sister in the back." Love is a fantastic feeling, but it's often blind and tends to cloud good judgment. It's beneficial for the narcissistic person to monopolize your time and secure your affection first, and get you involved in the relationship before your family and friends get a chance to get a good read about it and influence your opinion. They may also postpone introducing you to their family or friends so you don't unintentionally hear something about them that might sound some alarm bells or contradict the narrative and the person they've been portraying to you.

Strong family ties can be a challenge to the need and need for control of the pathological person. So, they can try to isolate you under the pretext of suggesting that both of you move in together or move to another city or state that will conveniently take you further away from your loved ones ' protection and support.

From the Frying Pan into the Fire

To make matters worse, the most effective way to strengthen and solidify the results of the positive reinforcement manipulation tactics is to start by incorporating negative reinforcement manipulation strategies while increasing the grasp of power over the target. The most effective way to motivate and maintain desirable habits is to create an unpredictable environment, which unexpectedly changes from one of love and concern (reward or gain) to callousness and cruelty (punishment or loss). The idea that using a random schedule of rewards and punishments is the most effective way to maintain behavior is called intermittent reinforcement and was introduced by a psychologist, B.F. Skinner. Skinner.

Often, when the narcissistic person incorporates negative conditioning techniques of affirmation into the relationship, he/she produces a traumatic bonding atmosphere that happens when the victim establishes fragile attachment bonds with their abuser. When the external factors of pain, anxiety, and fear are added to the mix, trauma bonds are established and reinforced. As the coercion moves from promises of incentives or benefits (positive reinforcement) to negative reinforcement (threats of punishment or loss), the severity increases and gives the victim feelings of anxiety and fear. The trauma bond is further reinforced when this occurs as the victim starts to see the narcissist or psychopath as the savior or remedy if he/she tries to ease the victim's fear or anxiety with temporary crumbs of love and concern.

Chapter 3: Covert Persuasion

Persuasion is convincing others to do something or to make others agree with your standpoint on a specific subject.

By employing effective persuasion methods, you can build a win-win situation. You pitch an idea in such a way as to make it impossible for others to refuse. You make an offer by applying lucrative cosmetics to it. It is not only a good deal or a position that makes sense to a particular person, but you can also embellish a less attractive idea in an efficacious and smart manner to achieve desired results. Some strategies can make your job more comfortable and make your case more convincing.

There are different techniques and tactics to help you persuade others with such skill that your actions are not practically measurable. They are discreet. The use of Covert Persuasion's resources in your personal and business life is not only ethical and appropriate, and it is vital for your overall success too.

Studies on Covert Persuasion

Covert Persuasion typically addresses the exact prediction of human behavior in any given context. Numerous attempts have been made in history to categorize people in an effort to understand them better and to anticipate their behavior. A brief overview of this initiative shows several of the most famous names in psychology, philosophy, NeuroLinguistic Programming (NLP), consumer behavior, and business From the days of Aristotle, Freud, Jung,

B.F. Skinner, Carl Rogers, William James, and Abraham Maslow to the more modern minds of psychology, industry, along with marketing; these great minds and others have come up with some brilliant ways of trying to understand our collective thought and decision making to persuade us and influence and direct our behavior.

The Hermann Brain Superiority Predictor, the Myers Briggs Type Indicator, , and the Language and Behavioral Profile are some examples of attempts to categorize us all. Of course, there are the endless personality tests that try to determine if you are well suited to a sales career. Besides these, there is the Enneagram of personality and, of course, the traditional4-quadrant description of us as a Thinker, Relater, Socializer, or Director.

There is a popular theory that all of our actions stem from our desire to avoid pain and attain pleasure. But it's not as easy as that. There's also the whole area of language analysis where it's assumed the words you're using will dictate your feelings. The labels (words) you put on your experiences determine your emotions. This study has a great history originating in the 1950s and has remained a strong set of principles to be used as a guide as you go forward and convince others to think your way. But even this theory, as useful as it is in some ways when evaluating others, is rife with an errant thought.

3.1 Effectiveness of Covert Persuasion

Everything you have or will ever get, become, do, or learn, you'll get with and through others. Life is but persuasion! The world is the perfect context for persuasion and convincing. Marketers and advertisers are making virtually endless attempts to understand every one of us accurately. Every year they will spend hundreds of millions of dollars trying to catch our attention, convince us to buy their product or service, sample their offer, vote for their candidate, and donate to their cause. In reality, if you live in the US, each year, you alone are the recipient of more than $3,200 of marketing and advertising messages. That's a lot of money that's invested in convincing people.

We've assembled a significant list of covert persuasion techniques to help you understand and apply these to achieve your goals in the real world. Starting with the self-talk inside your mind that is important for the trust required to manipulate others, all the way to the final act of communicating directly with the person you want to convince, your target person, it's all here.

Drawing from a wide cross-section of persuasion studies including experiments in social psychology, neuro-linguistic programming, language analysis, creative thinking, sales techniques, business communication skills, and personal communication skills, you'll discover startling new perspectives that will change the way you communicate forever.

Through mastering the powers of persuasion, you will find it easy to get more of what you want and when you want. If you are in sales, you will now have tools at your disposal, which will double or even triple your profits and commissions if you consciously and regularly put the ideas and techniques to use every day in your work life. It sounds insane, but you're not going to be in the first 1,000 to tell us this was what happened. If you're in business, you have to convince colleagues, managers, and superiors to go along with your proposals. Here you will find plenty of methods that you can use instantly to covertly persuade others to think your way.

3.2 How does Covert Persuasion Work?

Persuasion strategies also include phrases that are more convincing when it comes to your personal and business life. Combined in powerful stories, these terms will help you convince more people, more often.

However, the techniques of persuasion should be used ethically. Just as a hammer is designed to drive a nail through wood, but it can be misused to strike someone in the head, so these methods are designed to improve your persuasive power for good in both your professional and personal life, not for malicious or unethical results.

The strategies and techniques would encourage you to have more of what you want more often by subtly or covertly persuading the other person to think your way. It doesn't take any more time to achieve it;

however, you get everything you want, and you don't have to compromise or give up anything.

The methods of persuasion often consist of powerful hidden powers like emotions and the influence of well-structured, well-thought-out, result-based questions.

Covert Persuasion starts in the Mind. There are millions of words written about how the human brain works, and about just as many different opinions and hypotheses on how we think precisely. Yet, one thing is sure. To convince someone else to believe your way, you have to sync your mind with theirs. Effective persuasion begins and ends when a "mind meld" of real meaning, emotion, and comprehension is present. So how do we create this mind meld? How do we become more adept at persuading other people to think our way? The answer lies in knowing what motivates the other person and pushes him. Equipped with that experience, you can organize your thoughts and demands in such a way that other individuals with little or no questions can easily and quickly embrace them. They will see you as much as they do, and feel compelled to satisfy your requests.

The term covert persuasion means that covert things are not in plain sight. They are shielded, locked, and concealed from easy view. If we pair this with the act of convincing someone of something, we end up not being noticed by the target person(s) with our attempt of persuasion.

Covert Persuasion bypasses the vital human mind component without the message recipient being aware of the process. It is a question of getting through both resistance and response. This is achieved when one person sends a message, and the message is received from the recipient without any critical thinking or questioning.

Covert Persuasion is sometimes about controlling and handling the "state." What is the state of mind of that other person? For example, in the selling atmosphere, the consumer does not have to buy the product or service; in fact, purchasing is not an indication that there has been Covert Persuasion. An individual without money could easily be convinced and put in a state of purchase, but he did not have the money.

Ethics and Covert Persuasion

Some people ask whether' persuading' someone to do something is ethical. The easy answer is absolute, yes. It's not only ethical, but it's essential. Our economy (and our family and business) function because people are persuaded to buy. Millions of messages of communication are exchanged every single day, wittingly or unwittingly. All of these are designed to cause us to behave in some way.

Nonetheless, ethics always rests with the individual trying to persuade another. There are hundreds of specific techniques of persuasion that are not only effective but advance the cause of all when used ethically and responsibly.

Effective Suggestions ' Impact on Perception

Covert Persuasion is partially about creating change in your buyers ' or consumers ' minds without them actually being aware of the changes that are taking place. One of the most powerful tools to initiate this change in your customer's mind is to use the right words. The right words can change minds and lives when used at the right time.

In an experiment, Elizabeth Loftus (one of the world's leading memory researchers), performed in the 1970s, people viewed slides of a pedestrian-auto accident. A red Datsun slide (a sporty little car) was shown to them at a yellow Yield sign. The group was told, "Did you see another car passing by the Datsun at the stop sign? "Most of the community remembered a Stop sign rather than a Yield sign. The researcher's verbal knowledge, the words, and the query altered the memory of what they had seen.

When an authoritative figure gives a suggestion, it can often bypass a visual memory of a person to create a new and distinct memory. That means people will think differently depending on who's narrating an incident.

Our goal with Covert Persuasion is to create images that reinforce the behavior we want (to buy, seek, participate, vote, etc.) in the mind of the consumer. Using the right and most effective word combinations blended with the right questions leads to positive and intended thought and, eventually, the customer's behavior towards the goals we want is achieved.

Managing resistance by Omega Strategies

Distraction creates a receptive and easily persuaded

mind at moments of resistance. As we instinctively reject what we don't believe and feel the reaction to everything we fear, there is a strong need to help customers create new perceptions with new information to allow them to reach a unique outcome in their minds. The net result will be useful for you and the eventual selling of your product or service because you have helped the consumer create a new vision of what the future will look like.

The funny thing is that you want to counter the resistance before you paint those images. Whatever triggers the resistance or reaction (unconscious level resistance), you usually want to address it. In reality, most of the time, if you can't impede it, you have to answer it.

People are immediately receptive to knowledge and behaviors that are in line with their viewpoints. People can devise on - the-spot arguments against any opinion that is in direct conflict with their current belief. Also, identify existing beliefs and attitudes, so that these can be affirmed in some way. On the other hand, please don't make your customer state verbally anything that you might want him to change later. Once a mindset (orally or in writing) is conveyed, it will be retained even in the face of overwhelming evidence to the contrary. If people agree with the given perspective, dissent diminishes. The resistance is diminished with what the good doctors call "Omega Strategies." 'An Omega Strategy is a strategy of persuasion that does not try to boost or increase the product's value but is focused solely on the reaction and resistance in the persuasion process. One thing is for us to know that reciprocity is effective. It's quite another knowing how and when to cause reciprocity! Knowing that finding a favor can be an effective influencing strategy is different from knowing when to ask and how. We will try to teach you how to interact using a couple of different motivational methods persuasively, and we want to show you what not to do. "Boy, if you do that, you're going to kill yourself," Mom said, and the son went back to do it again— recall? Mom ignored a central driving factor that almost everyone forgets. Make a note to this. Provide specific instructions or steps while manipulating action or attempting to influence it. Simply asking someone to avoid doing something or "get a job" or "behave" or "shut up" is destined to fail utterly and entirely because these are not commands. Decades of research show that specific instructions are required to influence compliance and to encourage it. What does that mean to you? It means you need to step by step guide people through a process that leads them to the door that you eventually want them to open. Something short of doing this would probably not be useful in the short or long term.

3.3 Covert Persuasion Strategies

Some strategies can be used to persuade a person or group of people to do or act in a way you like. Let's go through the techniques.

Repetition

Speak to anyone who is well versed in the psychology of learning, and they will inform you that repetition is vital. It's also critical in persuasive writing, because if they don't get what you're saying they can't agree with you.

There are, of course, good repetitions and bad ones. To remain on the right side, make your point in many different ways, for example directly, using an example, in a story, through a quote from a famous person, and again in your review.

Reasoning

Recall the word's potential since psychological studies have shown that if you give them a reason why... even if that explanation doesn't make sense, people are more likely to answer a request. The strategy itself makes sense when you ponder over it painstakingly. We don't like being told stuff or asked to behave without a reasonable explanation. When you need people to be responsive to your thought line, always give reasons for this.

Consistency

It has been called the "hobgoblin of little minds," but consistency is an essential social characteristic in our thoughts and actions. We don't want to appear inconsistent, as this trait is associated with uncertainty and flightiness, whether reasonable or not, whereas consistency is associated with honesty and logical behavior.

Use this in writing by getting the reader to agree with something that would be hard for most people to disagree with beforehand. Then make your case rigorously, with plenty of supporting evidence, all while relaying your ultimate point back to the already agreed opening scenario.

Social Proof

Searching for other people's advice on what to do and embrace is one of the most powerful psychological forces in our lives. It can decide whether we are providing aid to a needy person, and it can determine if we dare to kill ourselves. Apparent examples of social proof can be found in testimonials and references beyond, and it is the driving force behind social media. But you can also effortlessly incorporate social proof elements into your writing, ranging from skillful cooperation with outside authorities to brazen dropping of the name.

Comparisons

The best friends of persuasive authors are metaphors, similes, and analogies. If you can succeed in relating your scenario to something the reader already recognizes as real, you are well on your way to getting someone to see things your way. But comparisons do work in other ways as well. Sometimes comparing apples to oranges (to use a familiar but powerful metaphor) will make you more persuasive Do not compare the price of your home study course with the price of a similar course — compare it with the price of a live seminar or the cost of your hourly consultation.

Agitate and Solve

This is a method of persuasion that acts as an overall approach to your case -making. First, you describe the problem and qualify your audience. Then you agitate the pain of the reader before giving your remedy as the answer, which will make everything better.
The process of inducing agitation is not about being sadistic. It is about empathy. There is an urge in you which is that you want the reader to know unequivocally that you accept his dilemma because you have dealt with it and are skilled in doing away with it. Your solution's reputation goes up if you show that you feel the pain of the prospect.

Prognosticate

Another element of persuasion involves giving the readers a glimpse into the future. If you can pose an extrapolation of current events in a convincing way into likely future results, you may also have a license to print money.

All of this approach is founded upon reputation. If you are fully aware of what you're talking about, then you're going to end up looking dumb. But if you can use your credentials or your explicit knowledge of the subject matter to back up your claims, this is an incredibly persuasive tactic.

Unification

Given our efforts to be intelligent and developed creatures, we humans are by nature exclusionary. Give someone a chance to be part of a group they want to be in— whether it's rich, trendy, or green or even contrary— and they're going to hop on board any train you're driving.

This is the technique used in the most important letter of sale ever published. Figure out what group people want to be in, and invite them to join while seemingly excluding others.

Address Objections

If you are arguing your case, and someone is left to think, "yeah, but..." well, you have failed. This is why direct advertisers use long copies— it's not because they want you to read all of it, it's because they want you to read enough until you buy.

It can be challenging to answer all the potential objections of at least the majority of your readers. Still, if you know your topic, the arguments against you should be reasonably obvious. If you do not think there are reasonable objections to your case, you are in for a surprise.

Storytelling

It is a catch-all technique — it can be used in conjunction with any of the previous nine strategies. The prime reason that the storytelling works so well is that it lies at the root of what is persuasion.
Stories allow people to persuade people, and that is what it is all about. You might claim we never persuade anyone of anything — we only help others determine individually that we're right. Do all you can to say better stories, and you will find that you are an incredibly convincing person.

Identification of problem

Identify a particular issue/problem. This is the thing the target doesn't want to encounter anymore. It could be high costs, high turnover of staff, spoilage of inventories, inadequate ads, almost anything that does not go well (and that your product or service is well suited to solving).

Extend Help

Help the customer discover that it would ultimately cost him/her in many unpleasant ways to continue with this issue/situation without fixing it. Behind that strategy is strong psychology. First hit the pain button, before you even start talking about possible solutions or how you, your company or your service can help.

Discover the Outcome Option

Have a desired outcome defined by your customers/clients. Making them opt for a better outcome is essential. Sometimes this is triggered by a simple question like: "What would you have liked to have happened?"And" Anything better than this?"Or" What would be your perfect outcome?

Identify the Consequences

Have your customers identify the impacts of this new outcome. This is very important in helping them to accept the new outcome. This move is also prompted by the questions you are going to ask. It could be often as simple as: "What would this new result mean to you and your business?"As they react, they form a new course of thinking that will lead them to your product or service.

Seek evidence

Verify that the selected outcome is the preferred one. Often customers/clients will tell you what they think you want to hear. This does not help anyone. They must not conceal anything and should tell the truth.

They must be frank with themselves and with you in order to follow true reliable conduct.

Stop being Judgmental

Don't be too quick to decide if you find a company or consumer reaction to being inappropriate. There is a strong possibility of different point of views between the two of you, as both of you are relatively new to each other's thought patterns. Take some time for clients to understand and connect. Once you do this, their answer may seem more important, and you may find that they agree with your message 100 percent.

Never Insult the Target

You must not blatantly point out to your target about his faulty decision. This is an echo of the old saying,

"The customer is always right!"This may not always be true, but in your mind, it's a good sign of caution. How would you feel if anyone told you that you were wrong? You'd probably become defensive and try to prove or demonstrate you're right. You'd end up sticking tighter to that point of view. You will respond the same way your customers do. Never tell them that they are incorrect or that last year it was a mistake to purchase your competitors ' product. Your customers would immediately ask whether it would be a mistake to buy from you.

Convert "No" into "Yes"

The reason that "no" comes out of people's mouths is because it's an instant reaction. They had done this or something like that before and so they quickly determined that it was a wrong decision.

"No" is an instant reaction, which means nothing. People don't know why they're saying "no." They don't understand why they're doing what they're doing, especially in hindsight, and they're going to perform opposite actions based on the terms that you're using in every conversation you've received. That is to say, people are entirely out of control until the persuasion expert walks in.

Imagine you are in a shower. The water suddenly turns cold. In the shower, you turn around and move the temperature up quickly. Yet, it's not going up. You find that hot water is being used in the kitchen!

You turn this off immediately. The 20-minute, soothing shower was ruined. You can remember the episode six months later as someone was incredibly rude, and that it was a bad shower. You do not remember the previous 20 minutes of relaxation you had in the shower. You take a five-minute shower the next day. It feels pleasant, soothing, and relaxing. But remember somebody's probably going to start using the hot water, so you get out pretty quickly, and it was a nice shower. Relaxing, if it's short! And you recall later that week that this was a nice shower. Every relation has ups and downs. A lot of your time is spent in house cleaning. You are not concentrating on your housewife relationship. Then you go through a period of arguing, fighting, and bickering with your spouse. It's a horrible time for a new relationship. The news is broken. Arguments are escalating. You had it already figured out! However, for the rest of your life, you tell people that you can't believe you stuck with that relationship for such a long period. If you want to figure out how to influence others, you need to know about people decision-making process, the influence of past experiences on present and future decisions, and their views about the future. Hence, this is what has been missing for many and what makes persuasion a "numbers game" for most.

People remember experiences, especially the awful ones. They certainly remember how things are going to be like. While asking about your competitor, elicit the peak experiences and the customer's ultimate experience. (They wouldn't see you if they were delighted.). When you attempt to change your customer's state of mind (if necessary), try to bring him to peak experiences. Also, make him remember that the last time he bought something was a brilliant purchase.

People do not know the future. It is very challenging for them to discover their probable reaction to an unknown future event. This is because that all of this is crucial in communication, persuasion, and obviously your business and relationships. People experience fear because they don't know the future. It's unknown realm. It's frightening. The usual response thus will be in negative until you bring them out there safely! This might be some of the most critical information you have ever learned. In one of the studies where people were having a critical colonoscopy, they were required to report at regular intervals of their discomfort level. The scope was not removed for one of the groups after the completion of process. However, the other group had the scopes removed a minute earlier (when the colonoscopy was finished) and with no additional minute of rest.

The group which remained attached to the scope for a longer time span found the process much comforting in contrast to the group which spent comparatively short time on the equipment. They also had a positive view and experience of colonoscopy. On the other hand, the group that had no spare moments of rest remembered it as much worse.

The research in persuasion is detailed. Your success lies in pointing out the possible outcomes beforehand. This is because the individual will be inclined to stick with whatever he perceives as logical. The experience and anxiety of losing is tough to get past without at least acknowledging and examining those possible outcomes. Then finish with a prominent and detailed view of a future outcome. You must remember to not paint it too rosy as it will result in failure.

We all know that the stock market crashed, the Titanic sank, the Twin Towers went down, but that is not a reason to avoid the stock market, boating, or tall buildings. In fact, having failed in the first twoquarters of the game should instigate you to work with more commitment and force in the remaining session of the game. You must communicate this message to your clients by using metaphoric language. You must not let a bad result in the past turn your client into a non-client.

Induce Fear

We all try to stay away from fear. We keep on trying to overcome and conquer our irrational fears. None of us wants to encounter frightening situations. Fear has the capability to motivate people better than any other thing. Having sex without condom can result in AIDS!" Can this statement induce fear or not? It could affect a change in your behavior, whereas in most of the cases it does not. The word "AIDS" has lost its power because of its widespread usage.

Just make a picture in your mind about the ultimate effect of smoking on your health and life. Just think that you are dead and your children and relatives are crying standing next to casket. This is a very frightening situation. Your face is dried, and they will never think of you in the same way." Instead, you should give him a set of instructions and advice for quitting smoking. You can ask him to gradually quit smoking first to half a pack per day and subsequently to one cigarette a day. This will be more effective and persuading than painting a very deadly scenario from the very beginning.

As regards cigarette smokers, they may have heard it 50,000 times, in which case they are immune against your plan and will not be paying attention to your advice. After using the same phrases or ideas over and over, the language becomes impotent. What should you do?

And is it ethical or not? That is an interesting question, and books about such issues have been written. A good thumb rule is to always act in the best interests of everybody that you work with.

Here, the lesson is simple If you are going to use fear in a communication to promote change or alter behavior or persuade someone to purchase your product, concept, or service, you must also include a collection of step-by-step guidelines in your message to make it successful.

Changing Beliefs

Beliefs stick like superglue in the brain as you try to persuade someone who believes something that is against your suggestion. You want your customers to buy you, your services, and the products you have. They have trust in you, your company, and the services you provide. You want to change things, and beyond a shadow of a doubt, you have proof that their opinion is incorrect and that the evidence you have is valid. If you give them the evidence, they won't buy from you, even if it's crystal-clear proof. You are facing an uphill task (if not impossible).

How uphill? You do know that people adhere to political parties and sects (the reason you are not supposed to talk about them in polite conversation) regardless of the facts to the contrary.

Political and religious convictions run deep because of their degree of protection against others who believe differently. The more beliefs that are preserved, the more they are rooted. As humans become emotionally intense about their convictions, they become more difficult to overcome from a logical mind with rationale or even undeniable facts that entirely banish the belief. Logic alone can rarely do away with a belief.

Covert Persuasion 101: The Techniques

Covert Persuasion consists of hundreds of strategies that have proved themselves. In any situation, not all tactics work. The decision is totally yours It is up to you to choose the ones that best suit you and your customer's needs.

One approach is building strong relationships with your audience. Essentially, this means making sure that they like you so much as an individual they can react to your message in a truly positive way.

One method of relationship building is sharing with the prospect a part of yourself. A bit of personal honesty and sincerity can go a long way toward building trust. When you take the time to find out what the other person is interested in and apply it to strengthen the bond between the two of you, you can use content to establish ties.

Another strategy is to coordinate with the other person or group. To put it another way, look, and act as much as you can like your client. People tend to love other people having similar traits. If you're dressed in business clothes, and the other person is in jeans and a t-shirt, the two could disconnect. Your speech, breathing, and posture can also be coordinated to match with the other person.

If the other person is angry, for example, and has an edge to his voice, don't try to cheer him up with a smile and pleasant story. This usually is not effective. If your target has an edge in his voice, even if only for a moment, let your voice have an advantage. This vocal timing will place you and your client in harmony. You will eventually lead your client out of his or her negative state and into a more responsive state of mind.

You can also match the speaking rate or words he speaks per minute. Yet, don't copy the target's verbal ticks. When he stutters or says "um" all the time, don't mimic him, or he will know you are using tactics to convince him, and the attempt will fail.

Another subtle technique is to synchronize your breathing with the target. This will place you at the same rhythm as your customer. The customer will hear the rhythm and will be more at home with you. Research shows that the bond between two people improves simply by timing another person's breathing, inhaling, and exhaling. Even if this is the only Covert Persuasion technique you use, the result holds; it's that effective.

Contrary to pacing the breathing of the other person, it is much easier to match someone's posture. But beware. He will feel uncomfortable if you assume the same body position and posture as your target. You want your customer to feel so comfortable that his defenses become less potent. But you don't want your customers to believe you're imitating them.

Once you are in sync with your client, you are ready to take the lead. Adjust your body language, the sound of your speech, speaking rate, or breathing. When he makes a similar gesture or changes his voice in the same way, you'll know the other person is watching you. Use a more confident tone in your voice as you direct your product into the conversation. If you find that the client follows your lead with a more positive voice, a higher speaking rate, and a more upper or lower tone of voice, you should feel assured that you have developed a relationship effectively.

If your target is in a "stuck state," and your attempt at persuasion doesn't work, get him to move around. Emotion can come from motion, and it's a proven fact. Stand up, walk around the room, or take lunch with the guy. By altering the physical position of the target, you can change the state of mind.

Another strategy involves fostering reciprocity. The whole relationship-building process is built based on empathy, compassion, care, commitment, and a desire for your client's well-being. Pacing and leading is a mechanism that provides confidence for you and your target as you move along at the right pace for your goal. The whole procedure can be as short as 20 seconds, or as long as one hour. The next step, after you've established a rapport is to develop your presentation.

Begin by giving something of the perceived value to your target. He would feel compelled to give back your generosity, either directly or by referring you to someone else.

You can also help the client solve a problem. Can you make a referral call for him? Could you help him expand his business by taking his 50 business cards? What can you do to motivate him that is beyond his expectations? Helping the other person creates a personal connection, making people feel secure enough to lower all their defenses.

Another useful tactic is to make a detrimental statement. That means recognizing a slight weakness or small flaw in the case that you create. It accomplishes two important things: First, it makes you look far more trustworthy.

Secondly, it helps your target to feel comfortable as you do the job of finding disadvantages in the proposal.

A similar strategy is to build credibility by giving the counter-argument some credit to the other side. It's all right to say the other companies are also making a good product. But while you recognize the value of the other commodity, you have every right to state — and prove — that yours is even better.

By pointing out a common enemy, you can get the target on your side too. There is nothing that unites two people like an enemy they have in common. Find the enemy of your target, and agree with his point of view. Was he abusive to IRS? Do the same people try to hurt both yours and his business?

There are three types of common enemies: First, there are enemies inside. All businesses are facing the rising costs of everything they purchase, and the constant pressure to sell more every day to cover those rising costs.

Second, external enemies like competition do exist. In a competing company or even another country, you may find a common enemy.

Third, personal enemies do exist. You may be able to form an alliance within the organization against a particular individual so that he does not advance.

Use the technique of sharing a short story about someone, just the way your client did. Create many stories about people who, in the past, have become your customers or have followed your business advice. Tell your target why the previous client reminds you of him or her. If the subject thinks the condition of the other person is close to his situation, he will imagine himself psychologically in your story. He will want to do what the person in the story has done, such as purchasing your product or agreeing with your idea.

You can also persuade people by using an astounding fact. Create the most valid claim you can make. You're making it easier for them to justify buying from you today by giving people new information, even though they've never bought from you in the past. They can feel comfortable making a new decision with the latest information.

Another main tactic for Covert Persuasion is building a reliable reputation. The best way of achieving this is to acknowledge the point-of-view of the other person, maybe saying something like: "I couldn't agree more with you in general." What you're doing is breaking down the prospect defenses". When he thinks you are basically in agreement with him, he can consider you are interested in a fair outcome. If the views of the prospect keep stopping him from accepting your point, then use the next tactic, one known as FFF. The letters allude to feel, felt and found. Here's an example of the same.

You say, "I understand how that makes you feel. Many of my colleagues once felt the same way. On the contrary, when they looked closer, they found a lot of sense, in my opinion.

FFF works because it establishes an emotional bond with your targets. It also means they're not the only ones who've felt the way they're doing, and that makes people feel better. Finally, the strategy helps prospects invest in finding a solution.

The strength of number three is yet another tactic to focus on. This includes the use of three points or presuppositions in a row. Look at it as a way to almost overpower the listener but do so in a controlled manner.

One of the three points should be right, and the others may be more open to discussion. Lead with a strong point, and the brain of the listener would begin to assume that there is veracity in all three points.

One strategy could qualify as the ultimate covert weapon: space utilization. This means making use of the immediate environment, including everything from what space you're in, to when the meeting takes place, to how close you're to someone else. This is just like someone being invited to the Oval Office by the President. People who visit it feel awed and humbled and that obviously reinforces the ability of the President to convince them.

So, at a time and place of your choosing, attain your goal. Always consider how the other person can feel at ease with your body language. Above all, do not physically get too close to your prospect. Think about how uncomfortable it is in a crowded elevator in that way.

The strength of humor is another technique. If your mutual fund has a track record over the past 10 years of a 12 percent return per year, then understate that by saying, "Now, if you average 10 percent per year. ."... Your investment has received a profit of 12 percent over 10 years, but you are cautious for your client, and he understands and appreciates it.

Another way of persuading consumer to use numbers is to be precise and then beat the accuracy. When you know, for example, that a particular car will get your customer 19 miles per gallon, tell him this. Then tell him a secret: "But if you're using a certain oil brand, you can add an extra three miles per gallon of gas, and that translates into hundreds of dollars savings per year." Being precise adds credibility and legitimacy to your whole statement. Unconsciously, people feel better when they hear very specific information, instead of round numbers.

What's more, everyone is looking for solutions that save time and effort. And vow to get that all done quicker, faster, and healthier. Combine all three guarantees for a boundless bid. For example, "You're going to get it this afternoon instead of next week, and I'm responsible for getting all the work done, so you don't have to, and the outcome will be much better than it was." Ultimately, using hypnotic language patterns is one of the most effective strategies. To use this tactic, state what you want the person to do, but precede the instruction with words that make it sound like you don't tell the person what to do. Consider these examples:' I wouldn't advise you to buy this car; that's your choice." I wouldn't tell you to invest more money in stocks; you have to find that out on your own." You don't have to invest in several funds; one or two is just fine." I don't know if you believe you should decide now, so you don't miss out.' Try using phrases like these in as many different work environments as possible. People will start answering more of your requests than they have ever done in the past.

The Keywords of Covert Persuasion

Some phrases are much more convincing than others regardless of the techniques you use, and they are the ones you should use in your commercials and conversations.

The 12 most convincing words in English are You, Money, Save, Outcomes, Health, Simple, Love, Discovery, Proven, Fresh, Security, and Guarantee. These 12 words evoke powerful emotions. They attract the attention and interest of men.

Some important words in marketing include Your, Free, Yes, Quick, Where, Secrets, Sell, Now, Transform, Energy, Advertise, Benefits, Exciting, Science, Technology, and Solution.

Often, when answering a customer's request, use the powerful word "because," and you'll find people much more likely to agree with you. The term "because" establishes a causal relationship, a link between one thing and another, and those who follow it in a sentence.

Here are some examples of how strong words might be used.

"This proven scientific method contains three easyto-use strategies that will change your life." Another example is: "Do you want to save money?"A third example is:" How do you want to discover the secrets of this exciting new technology?"The idea is to use terms that resonate with the clients and prospects.

The Keys to Using Covert Persuasion in a Story

In this segment, we'll explore how storytelling can influence people.

Coherent stories have more than just a start, middle, and end. They also have a point— or a moral point — and this can serve as a robust persuasive instrument. Covert Persuasion is very well represented in stories. This makes the story more likely to get its intended outcome: persuading others to share your thought. Sadly, most stories struggle to be convincing due to lack of emphasis and therefore appear to be rambling and meaningless.

The critical point in every meaningful communication is to catch and focus the attention of the audience. To do this, you need to share information in a clear, convincing manner that appeals to the innate curiosity of individuals. It is essential to have knowledge of the following factors when using a story to make your case.

First, you have to have an idea, a reason you're telling a specific story. Would you say it to make the person laugh, or persuade him you're clever or sell him on your idea?

Second, decide what you want the other guy to think or feel. You will want him to know, for example, that you are interested in his problem and you have helped other people with the same problem. Third, know your intention to be with a specific person or group. For this particular story, this is not the same as your intention. It is the point why you are with this person. What is your purpose of reassuring him that you're honest, involved, concerned and that you want him to succeed? Fourth, infuse powerful self-revelations into the plot. This is important because you need to express your values and beliefs. Relate the story to their experiences.

The stories you tell are meant to be about yourself and past clients. However, covertly, you must ensure that the tale is also of great interest to the listener. You tell the story because the listener wants to know who you are. If executed properly, Self-revelation will build confidence.

Fifth, to catch the attention of the crowd, address a topic they would passionately agree with you on. Subjects might include reducing costs, investing in the future, adding new customers, or maintaining existing ones.

Sixth, describe exactly how your product or concept affects your company or quality of life directly. Great products— from computers to cell phones— are saving time and improving lives.

Seventh, let the listener know you're fantastic but be modest. Don't tell people you're either smart, trustworthy, or considerate. In your story, cite someone else who said to you that you're wise, honest, or kind. For example, "The customer told me,' You're fantastic. I have never encountered such excellent service."

Eighth, explain how other consumers have gained success from using your product or service — in transparent, realistic, and verifiable words. Maybe they have dramatically increased profitability or income, or reduced employee turnover or increased customer retention.

Don't tell a story unless it places you within a context that the viewer can relate to. The goal for you is to have the audience nodding their heads and saying, "Yeah, I'm a great lot like the speaker." Telling a story that catches the imagination of the audience is a successful way to convince — and sell. One method of persuasion is the use of relevant questions, and that is the subject of the next segment.

Using Questions to Covertly Persuade

The whole trick of persuasion is to help the other person create his or her idea–which is, of course, your personal opinion. You're making him say it, own it, and consequently, he'll act on it.

Using The Factor of Availability is a simple tactic for getting people to own an idea. What this signifies is that the judgment of a person is clouded by what is most at your fingertips.

In the extensive reporting of plane crashes, we see The Availability Factor at work. It causes people to have an inordinate fear of air travel— even if it is the safest form of transportation. In fact, a donkey is statistically more likely to kick you to death than to die in a plane crash. But we don't see or hear many stories of people dying like this, so we're more scared of flights than we're afraid of donkeys.

Convincingly, what you are trying to do is make your commodity, circumstance, or concept highly accessible to your prospect. One way of doing this is through media and advertising, and another is through personal conversation, which employs the use of questions.

People often interrupt during answering questions because they were taught to be polite, and it's considered rude to miss a request. That's why you feel compelled to respond, even if you're in the middle of a meaningful conversation, and someone interrupts you by asking about the time. Participants also want to answer questions to prove they are competent.

There are 10 essential things that a salesperson can do with questions.

- First, they divert the focus of a person and get immediate attention.
- Second, they put the audience in an open-minded mood.
- Third, they make the audience use his terms.

- Fourth, they help to generate interest in your subject.
- Fifth, they minimize resistance to ideas by exposing them
- Sixth, they direct listeners towards the desired conclusion.
- Seventh, they allow you to give credit to listeners for the quality of their thinking.
- Eighth, they enable you to bypass distractions, because follow-up questions help you keep your audience on track.
- Ninth, they help you take the edge off the sales pitch, because questions involve the customer in making the decision.
- Tenth, they build your self-confidence in your ability to start and control a conversation. If you comply with the rules pertaining to questions you will have these positive effects.

One rule is that you shouldn't ask questions if you aren't pretty sure what the answer will be. Above all, don't ask people highly technical questions where they may get embarrassed because they don't know the answer.

Another rule is to use leading questions whenever possible. These questions lead the listener toward the conclusion you want. For example, "Most people are buying the red ones because of their availability. Hence, you'd probably like a red one too, right?" People will first silently answer your questions in their own minds. Your task is to let your audience lead themselves into the course of action you want them to take. Once they start this process, they will start agreeing. You have entered and directed their minds with questions, and they will change their own minds with their answers.

Following three questions will help you to take control of your target's brain:

1.   Have you ever wondered how to get a better product at a lower price?

2.   What's most important to you in this kind of product?

3.   In what ways would this product make your work easier?

Fifteen Observations About People and Covert Persuasion

You can't sell effectively to specific people if you start out with unrealistic assumptions about humanity in general. Undoubtedly, there are exceptions to all generalizations, but most people share certain characteristics and imperfections.

Human nature sometimes helps in your persuasive efforts, but in other cases it can work against you. Here are 15 observations about people that will help you to use Covert Persuasion more effectively:

1.   Most of the time people have no knowledge of how to ask important questions. This is partly because they'd rather pretend they already know the answer. To overcome this tendency, develop good questions to help guide prospects in the right direction.

2.   Another factor is that people let their bad attitudes, developed over time, cloud their current judgments. Your approach should be to inject into your conversation potent questions that can align with the prospect's viewpoint. For example, you might ask a resistant customer: "Did you know there's a new technology that overcomes the problem you've highlighted?"

3.   People need help to visualize. To make it easier for them, use metaphors and analogies to connect your product or idea with something familiar to the customer.

4.   People know what they don't want. Your task is to direct the process toward what they do want but find it challenging to express it. One of the worthremembering phrases is, "I am aware of the fact that you don't have knowledge of this particular thing but would it's knowledge have made any difference! You will be surprised to discover an overwhelming response to the said question.

5.   Speed is the key to getting the job. Sometimes the customer will say yes if you can deliver what they want quickly. Force yourself to get it done in less time, by asking yourself, "What are seven ways I can get it done faster?"

6.   Customers would rather take their business elsewhere than complain about a bad experience with your product. In that case, you must become super-sensitive to the treatment your clients are receiving. Ask them what would make the situation better.

7.   Prospective clients have no knowledge of as how your product can resolve their issues. Therefore,

it's your job to find out what customers need — and once you know what they need, recommend a solution.

8. People have internal gauges, a feeling or instinct that tells them when something's not right. The goal of selling should be to use persuasion to ensure that the customer 's internal gauges tell him or her to buy.

9. Some prospects are time wasters. They're the ones you should politely refer to competitors. Make them someone else's headache, and concentrate on the people who are worth your time.

10. Most of the time people have a sense of ownership. They approach businesses with the same attitude. Your success is to respond to everyone with honesty and fairness.

11. Perception is reality. The way you see the world might differ greatly from a client's view. Ask questions that will help you to understand his perspective.

12. People are prone to laziness always in search of easy ways of doing things. This could mean that if it's not easier to buy from you, there will be no transaction. You have convinced them. You need to prove to them that why and how a particular transaction can relieve them of a big problem. You need to help them in every manner. However, if you require your prospects to do too many things, they will never become your customers.

13. People tend to do more to get rid of pain. They do not seek pleasure in doing anything. You have to

give proof to the prospect of what he will lose if he doesn't take action now.

14.   People are not good listeners. On the contrary, they prefer to express themselves. This can hold true for you too. You must use questions to steer the conversation. And listen more than you talk.

15.   People   overpromise   and   under   deliver. Companies   usually   have   good intentions. However, they fail to inculcate a sense of exclusivity in the customer. They fail to deliver in accordance with the promises made earlier on. You should avoid doing the said. You must promise less and deliver more. In doing so you'll pleasantly surprise your customers, and they'll tell everyone they know.

Putting it All Together

Not everyone works in sales, but we all sell something every day. Although you might not be selling products or services, you might be selling your ideas, your viewpoints, and most of all, yourself — as an honest, caring, informed individual.

So, let's put together all the information we've covered. Remember, the fundamental goal of Covert Persuasion is to move your target person from where he is to where you want him to be.

To help you stay focused, make a worksheet before you meet with a client, colleague, or anyone else you want to persuade. Start by writing down your selfish goal: What exactly do you want as a perfect outcome?

Next, list everyone involved, and where they are starting from: Are they skeptical about your product or idea, open-minded, or eager to agree with you? Then, list what you want them to believe, feel, and do as a result of your persuasion.

Be sure to use the right words, questions, and stories to deliver your message. Remember the power of words like You, Money, Save, Results, Health, Easy, Love, Discovery, Proven, New, Safety, and Guarantee.

Direct the other person's thinking by using questions such as, "In what ways would this product make your work easier?" Don't forget that when you ask a question, you are in control of the thought processes of the other person.

Take advantage of the hypnotic language patterns, such as "I wouldn't tell you to. . ." "You don't have to. . ." and "You might want to. . ."

Finally, go through all of the Covert Persuasion tactics, and choose the ones you are going to use. That's why you'll want to refer to this summary again and again, so you can stay familiar with all the tricks and techniques.

When you use Covert Persuasion, the other person won't have any conscious idea that you are persuading him. He will feel ownership of the decisions you lead him to make. And, as we know, people feel more committed to decisions they make than to anything you tell them. This is extremely critical. Since you don't want to just win the sale; you want to win a lifetime customer.

Chapter 4: Brainwashing

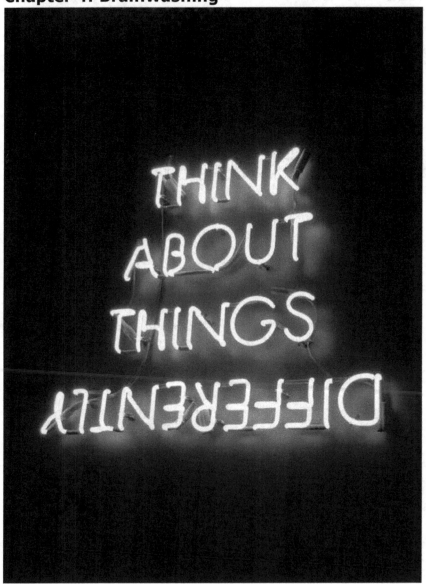

This chapter will concentrate on the brainwashing process and all the components that come with it. Through the media and the films shown, many people see brainwashing as an unethical activity performed by those who try to manipulate, control and gain power. Some who genuinely believe in the power of brainwashing claim people are trying to manipulate their minds and actions all around them. The brainwashing method often takes place in a much more subtle way and does not include the malevolent activities that most people associate with it. This chapter will go into much more depth about what brainwashing is, and how it can affect the way of thinking of the subject.

4.1 What is Brainwashing?

Brainwashing will be discussed in terms of its use in psychology. Brainwashing is referred to as a means of transforming thinking through social influence. This sort of social influence happens to every person throughout the day, regardless of whether or not they know it. Social influence is the set of techniques used to alter the habits, values, and attitudes of other people. For example, compliance procedures that are used in the workplace may potentially be considered a form of brainwashing because when you are on the job, they force you to act and think in a particular way.

Brainwashing, in its most severe form, can become more of a social issue as these methods work to change the way someone thinks without the subject consenting to it.

For brainwashing to work effectively, due to its invasive impact on the subject, the subject will need to go through complete isolation and dependency.
This is one of the reasons why many of the instances of brainwashing believed to occur in totalistic cults or prison camps. The brainwasher, or the operator, must have complete control over their subject matter. It means they have to monitor the eating habits, sleeping patterns, and meeting the subject's other human needs, and none of these actions will occur without the agent's will. The agent must work during this cycle to gradually break down the entire identity of the subject to make it no longer function properly. After losing the identity, the agent must seek to substitute it with the desired values, attitudes, and actions.

The brainwashing mechanism is still up for debate as to whether it will succeed or not. Some psychologists hold the belief that a person can be brainwashed as long as there are proper conditions. The whole thing isn't as dangerous as it is portrayed in the media, however. Since there are different definitions of brainwashing, this make the assessment of the brainwashing influence on the subject more difficult. Some of those definitions require some threat to the subject's physical body for it to be perceived as brainwashing.

When you follow this description, then even certain extremist cult activities would not be considered correct brainwashing as there is no physical abuse.

Many definitions of brainwashing would rely on control and coercion without physical power to bring about the change in the subjects ' beliefs. Either way, experts believe that the consequence of brainwashing is only a short-term phenomenon, even under the ideal conditions. They conclude that with practice, the subject's old identity is not wholly eradicated; instead, it is put further into the subconscious and will return once the new identity is no longer enhanced.

Robert Jay Lifton came up with some exciting thoughts about brainwashing in the 1950s following his study of Chinese and Korean War camp prisoners. During his research, he concluded that the brainwashing of these prisoners was a multistep process. The process started with assaults on the prisoner's sense of self and ended with a suspected change in the subject's beliefs. In the subjects he researched, Lifton identified 10 steps for the brainwashing phase. These included:

• Attack on the subject's identity

• Forcing guilt on the subject

• Forcing the subject into self-deception

• Achievement point

• Offering leniency to the subject if they change

• Compulsion to confess

- Channeling guilt in the intended direction

- Releasing the subject of presumed guilt
- Progressing to harmony

- Final confession before a rebirth.

Additionally, the entire procedure has to be executed in an isolated environment. It ensures that all the typical social references used by the subject are impossible to come into contact with. Therefore, mental clouding strategies will be used to accelerate processes such as malnutrition and sleep deprivation. While this may not be true of all cases of brainwashing, there is often a presence of some physical harm, which contributes to making it difficult for the subject to think independently and critically as they would normally.

Steps Used

While Lifton divided the steps of the brainwashing process into 10 steps, it is structured in three stages by modern psychologists to understand better what's going on for the subject during this process. Such three steps involve breaking down the self, incorporating the concept of redemption into the subject matter, and restoring the subject's ego.

A proper understanding of each of these stages, and the process that happens with each of them will help you know what happens during this process to the subject's identity.

Breaking Down of Self

Breaking down of the self is the first stage of the brainwashing cycle. The consultant wants to break up the subject's old identity during this process. He wants to make them feel more vulnerable and open to the desired new identity. This move is necessary to carry on the process.

The agent will not be very productive with their efforts if the subject stays firmly affixed to its resolve and its old identity. Breaking the identity and making the individual doubt the things around them can make it more comfortable in the later steps to bring about a change in identity. This is achieved through several phases, including assaulting the subject's personality, bringing on guilt, self-betrayal, and then reaching the breaking point.

Assault on Identity

The attack on the subject's identity is essentially a systemic assault on the self-sense of the subjects or their ego or personality, along with their core belief system. It involves the subject questioning their identity and the validity of their past knowledge. The agent will spend a lot of time denying all that matters for the subject. For example, in prison camps, the agent will say things like "You're not defending freedom," "You're not a man," and "You're not a soldier." For days to months, the topic will be under constant attacks like these. This is done to fatigue the subjects into becoming disoriented, confused, and exhausted. When the subject enters this sort of state, their convictions may begin to appear less intense, and they may start to believe the things they are told.

Guilt

Once the subject has gone through their identity assault; they will enter the stage of guilt. The target is always told they are bad as they go through this new identity crisis that has been brought on. This is done to bring the subject under a great sense of guilt.

The subject shall remain under an unabated attack for any of the things they've done, no matter how big or small the actions might be. The nature of the attacks can also vary; the target could be attacked in the way they dress because of their belief systems, and even because of their slow eating. Over time, the subject will start feeling guilt all the time around them, and they'll feel all the things they're doing are wrong. This can help make them feel more comfortable and will possibly go along with the new identity that the agent wants to produce.

Self-Betrayal

Now that the subject is led to believe they are evil and all their acts are unacceptable, the agent will try to compel the subject to realize they are evil. At this point, the subject drowns in his guilt and feels very disoriented. This enables the agent to force the subject to denounce his old identity through the continuance of the mental assaults, the threat of some tremendous physical damage, or a combination of the two.

Usually this is accomplished by doing a wide range of things like getting the target to criticize their colleagues, relatives, and family who follow the same system of belief as he does. While this cycle will take a while to occur, the subject may feel like he has deceived everyone he was once committed to. That will also increase the guilt as well as the loss of identity already felt by the target, further breaking down the subject's identity.

Breaking Point

This is where the subject feels extremely crippled and disoriented. We might ask questions like Where am I? Who am I, then? So, what do I do? At this point, the subject is in an identity crisis and is going through some profound humiliation. Since they have betrayed all the values and the people he has always known, a nervous breakdown is going to occur on the subject.

In psychology, this simply means a series of severe symptoms that often suggest a large number of suspected psychological disorders. Some of the signs may include general disorientation, severe depression, and excessive sobbing. The subject can feel lost entirely, along with a loose grip on reality. Once the subject hits this breaking point, they will have lost their sense of themselves. It is at this very; the agent will be able to do pretty much whatever they want with them as the subject has lost their understanding of what is happening around them and who they are.

Even at this stage, the agent must set up the different temptations needed to convert the subject into a new system of beliefs. This new system will be set up in a manner that gives the subject relief from the suffering they experience.

Possibility of Salvation

It is time to move on to the next step after the agent has been successful in breaking down the subject's self. This step includes giving the subject the chance of salvation only if they are willing to turn away from their former system of belief and ready to embrace the new one that is being offered. The subject is given the opportunity to realize what's around them, they're told they'd be healthy again, and they'd feel better if they just followed the appropriate new path. There are four phases in this stage of the brainwashing process; leniency, a compulsion to confession, channeling of guilt, and releasing of guilt.

Leniency

Leniency is the' I can help you' phase. By the time the subject reaches this stage, he has been broken down and forced to move away from the people and the convictions they have held on to for so many years. They've been told they're evil and all they do is wrong. The subject would feel lost and lonely in the world, ashamed at all the bad things they've done and wondering which way to turn around.

The agent can offer them some sort of relief when they reach this stage by extending a helpful hand to the subject.

It can typically be in the form of a respite from the violence suffered by the subject, or some other little kindness. For instance, the agent may give the subject a little extra food or drink of water. The agent might even take a few moments to ask personal questions from the subject about his home and loved ones. Such petty acts of kindness will seem like a big deal to subject in his current state, resulting in the subject feeling of a great sense of gratitude and relief towards the agent. Such emotions are often far out of proportion as compared to the offer that has been made. In some cases, the subject can believe that the agent has done the act of saving their lives instead of providing just a small service.

The manipulation of events appears to work in the agent's favor, as the target will now establish loyalty relations with the agent rather than past things.

Compulsion to Confession

They will try to get a confession out of the said procedure only when the agent has been able to gain the trust of their subject. This stage is often referred to as the "You can help yourself." During this stage of the brainwashing, the subject starts to see the discrepancies between the pain and guilt they experienced during the assault on identity and the satisfaction they experience from the unexpected leniency that is offered. If the process of brainwashing is successful, the subject might even start to feel a desire to reciprocate some of the kindness to the agent. Once this occurs, the agent will be able to present the concept of confession as a possible means of relieving the subject from the pain and guilt they experience.

Then, the subject will be guided through a cycle of confessing all the wrongs and sins they have committed in the past.

Such errors and sins will, of course, be in relation to how they affect the new identity that is being created For instance, if the subject is a prisoner of war, this move would encourage them to admit the wrongs that they have done by defending freedom or battling the other country's regime. Even if these are not explicitly wronging or crimes, they go against the new ideology that the government is always right and must be confessed as such.

Channeling of Guilt

The subject enters the channeling of guilt phase after they have been subjected to self assault for several months. By the time the subject reaches this point in the process of brainwashing, they will feel the guilt and the humiliation that has been put on them, but by this time, it has lost its meaning.

They can't tell you exactly what they did wrong to make them feel this way; they know they are wrong.

The agent will be able to use the subject's blank slate to describe why they find themselves in the pain they experience. The agent will be able to attach the sense of guilt to the subject. If the agent wants to change a belief system, they will take on the old system and persuade the subject that those past beliefs are the reason for the present guilt. This is the stage where the bond is formed between the old beliefs and the new beliefs; primarily, the old belief system has been established to correlate with the psychological pain that the subject experienced while the new belief system has been established to create the ability to escape that agony. The choice is going to be the subjects, but it's pretty easy to see that they're going to select the new system to get better.

Releasing Guilt

The subject has come to realize in this phase that their old values and beliefs are causing them pain. By this time, they're worn down and tired of feeling the guilt and shame that's been put on them for months. They begin to realize that what they have done is not actually something that makes them feel this way; instead, it is their convictions that are triggering the shame. The accused subject can feel some satisfaction from the fact that they can do something about the culpability. They'll probably feel relieved because they've come to understand that they're not the bad person, they're the people they've been around and their belief system that's the real culprit that triggers the malaise they can address to get healthy again. The subject has discovered that they have a way of escape, which is by separating from the corrupt system of beliefs they have maintained and accepting the new one that is being offered.

All that the subject will have to do is to remove the remorse they feel by detaching them from the institutions and people associated with the old belief system.

The subject now has some power over this point. They will be able to realize that it is up to them to release the guilt entirely. To be freed from the wrongness, all the subject will have to do for this stage is to confess to any of the deeds that they have committed during their association with the old belief system. When complete confession is made, the subject will have achieved the full psychological rejection of its former identity. At this stage, the agent will need to step in to give the subject a new identity and help them rebuild their identity into the desired one.

Rebuilding Self

The subject has already gone through a lot of steps and emotional turmoil before this phase. They've been put through an ordeal that's supposed to rob them of their old identity by telling them they're evil and need to be fixed, and have eventually come to realize that their belief system is the root of their wrongdoing and that it needs to be changed. If all of this is achieved, the subject will need to learn, with the aid of the counselor, how to reconstruct their selves. Each stage allows the agent to incorporate the ideas of the new system as the subject is like a clean slate and very keen on learning how to be better and feel better. This stage or phase is composed of two steps, which are harmony and the final confession before starting again.

Harmony

This move will be used by the agent to persuade the subject that making a change should be their preference.

We should tell the subject that they have the choice of choosing what is right and that making a change will help them feel better. The agent will then explain and subsequently implement the new belief system in a way that makes it the right choice for the subject. The agent should stop the abuse during this stage, and instead make a point of offering mental calm and physical support to the subject. The point of doing this is to reconcile the old beliefs with the pain and suffering while adding joy and comfort to the new beliefs.

This stage is set up in such a way that the subject has the option of which route to take even though it is not really up to them. The subject has to use this stage to choose between old beliefs and new beliefs to decide effectively how they will behave for the rest of their lives. By this point, the subject has already gone through the process of rejecting their old beliefs because of the leniency and suffering they have endured.

Because of this, they are relatively likely to make the option for the new belief system to alleviate their guilt. The new identity that has been introduced is attractive and secure because it is entirely different from the old identity that in earlier steps had contributed to the breakdown. Using reasoning and considering the relevant state of mind of the subject, it's easier to see that the new one is the only identity the subject will choose for their peace of mind and protection.

Final Confession and Starting Over

Although the option is not theirs at all, the agent has worked all the time diplomatically to make the subject feel like they have the free will to choose the new identity. If the process of brainwashing is done correctly, the subject will objectively think about the new options and decide that the best one is to take on the new identity. The subject has been conditioned to think this way, and it is the one that makes the most sense in their current state of mind. There are no other choices; they can be released from the shame and embarrassment they feel only by opting for the new identity as they have found that preferring the old identity leads to pain and guilt. If the subject rejects the new identity for some reason, there would be backtracking in the entire process of brainwashing, and they would be forced to undergo it all over again so that the desired results could be achieved.

During this stage, the subject gets to decide they're going to choose good, meaning they're going to decide to go with the new identity.

When the subject compares their old identity's torment and pain with the peacefulness, which comes with the new, they will always choose the new identity. This new identity is something of a sort of salvation.

It's the thing that helps them feel good, as they no longer have to struggle with remorse and unhappiness. When this stage approaches its legitimate end, the subject must abandon their old identity and go through a process of pledging loyalty to their new one, believing it will serve to make their lives better.

During this final stage, there are many ceremonies and rituals that take place. The change from the old identity to the new identity is a big deal since there's been a lot of time and effort made from both sides for the said purpose.

The subject is usually inducted into the new community during these ceremonies and welcomed with the new identity. For some brainwashing victims, during this time, there is a sense of rebirth. You are encouraged to accept your new identity and are welcomed into the new community with open arms.

Rather than being lonely and alone, there are many new friends and members of the community on your side. Instead of feeling the remorse and agony that has plagued you for many months you'll feel happiness and peace with all that's around you. The new identity now belongs to you, and the process of brainwashing is complete.

This may take place over several months to even years. Many people are set in their identity and the beliefs they have; all of this can't be changed in just a few days unless the person is already willing to change as otherwise, the brainwashing techniques would be pointless.

Isolation would also be necessary because outside factors in this cycle would prevent the subject from relying on the agent.

That is why most of the cases of brainwashing take place in prison camps and other isolated places. Thus, the vast majority of people will not have the chance to encounter brainwashing because they are always surrounded by people and technologies that would hamper the whole process of brainwashing.

Once the person is isolated due to the many steps that must be taken to alter the values held by the individual for many years, the transition takes a long time so that they embrace the new identity as theirs. At the same time, they must realize that they have not been compelled to opt for the choice.

It is fairly obvious from the above that there are quite a few steps required to go through the process of brainwashing. It's not something that can happen simply by running into someone on the street and exchanging a couple of words. It needs time and isolation to persuade the subject that all they know is wrong and that they are a terrible person. It then carries on with efforts to force out a confession that the subject is bad and that they want to give up all the things they have done that are bad because of their old identity. Eventually, the subject will be led to believe that by abandoning their old ideas and embracing new ideas they can bring about a positive and better change in their identity.

For the brainwashing to be successful and the new identity to be created, all of these measures must occur.

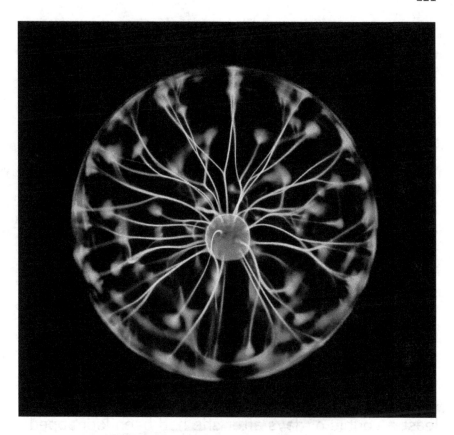

4.2 Brainwashing and Court Defense

Throughout history, people have claimed to have done horrific wrongs because they were brainwashed. It was an excuse for many to pretend to save their own lives or to get away with mass murder or some other human crime. It could even be something as simple as stealing from someone else. Whatever the crime was, brainwashing was an easy defense because it took away the blame for the action from the victim, and it was challenging to prove if someone was brainwashed or not.

Whether pleas for brainwashing can be used in court as a defense is subject to some debate. Most experts believe that bringing this defense into the courtroom will overwhelm the courts with false brainwashing claims, and it would be a burden on court resources for proving or disproving this defense. Notwithstanding this, several cases have been brought before the court, which can illustrate the legitimacy of brainwashing as a defense for crimes committed.

The first such example occurred in 1976. Patty Hearst, the heiress of a huge publishing fortune, used brainwashing as a defense when she stood for trial for a bank robbery. In the early 1970s, the SLA, the Symbionese Liberation Army, abducted Hearst and he eventually joined the organization. Hearst told the court that she had been locked up in a closet for at least a couple of days after she had been kidnapped. While in the closet, Hearst said she hated her life, was brutalized, exhausted, and underfed while SLA leaders bombarded her with their ideology against a capitalist country. Within two months of her abduction, Patty had changed her name while also issuing a statement saying her family was "pigHearst's" and then appeared on a bank's security tape, robbing it along with those who kidnapped her.

Patty Hearst stood for this bank robbery trial in 1976 and was defended by F. Lee Bailey. It was claimed in the defense that the SLA had brainwashed Hearst. The brainwashing had forced Hearst to commit a

123

crime she would never have committed under any other circumstances. She could not differentiate between the good and the bad during the said mental state, that is, when she was under the effects of brainwashing, and therefore should not be found guilty of bank robbery. The court disagreed with this reasoning and instead found her guilty and sentenced her to seven years if imprisonment. However, a few years later, President Carter commuted her sentence so that she only ended up spending a total of two years in prison.

Lee Boyd Malvo Case

The Lee Boyd Malvo case is yet another well-known brainwashing defense case. The case used brainwashing to defend insanity, and it ended up about 30 years after the Patty Hearst trial in the courtrooms. Lee Boyd Malvo was on trial in 2002 for the role he played in the sniper attacks that took place in Washington D.C. Malvo, who was 17 at the time, and John Allen Muhammad, 42, ended up killing ten people and wounding three during the rampage. The argument used for this prosecution was that Muhammad had brainwashed the young Malvo so that he could commit the crimes. Just as in the Hearst trial, the defense argued that if he had not been under Muhammad's influence, Malvo would not have committed those crimes.

The story concocted by the defense was that Malvo lost the warmth of his mother when he was only 15 years old. It was then that Muhammad met the boy and, in 2001, took him to the USA.

At the time, Muhammad was an army veteran and was trying to fill the teen's head with dreams of an imminent race war. To this end, Malvo had been trained as a professional shooter. During the process, Muhammad isolated Malvo from others while being steeped in Islam's vitriolic and idiosyncratic brand that Muhammad followed along with a strict diet and exercise routine. All of this on the young Malvo is thought to have been part of the brainwashing process.

The defense argued that Malvo had been brainwashed because of his time spent with Muhammad, and because of that, he was unable to tell what was right out of what was wrong. Malvo was found guilty despite the prosecution efforts and was awarded a life sentence in prison without any chance of parole. Muhammad was sentenced to the death penalty in a separate trial.

So far, brainwashing does not seem to gain much ground in the courts as a form of defense.

To start with, proving that a defendant was brainwashed in the first place is much too tricky.

Next, it's improbable anyone will have been brainwashed. Instead, the prosecution will use it as a way to get a lighter sentence. Furthermore, the idea of brainwashing has always been viewed as utterly ridiculous by many juries.

Eventually, this defense probably won't stand much chance in the courtroom.

4.3 Brainwashing Techniques

Brainwashing is not always as extreme as what has been described in this chapter. The mentioned methods are used for true brainwashing" and are rarely done to the subject. There are many other kinds of brainwashing that do occur on a daily basis. They might not work to get you to give up your old identity entirely and thus embrace a new one, but they do work to help change your thoughts and ideas about what's happening around you. This segment will concentrate on some of the techniques that are often used during brainwashing irrespective of the fact whether they can be referred to as true brainwashing or not.

Hypnosis--Hypnosis shall be explained in considerable detail in the next chapter can sometimes be construed as a type of brainwashing. Hypnosis is essentially the induction of a high suggestibility state. This state is often cleverly disguised as meditation or relaxation.

The practitioner is able to suggest ideas to the subject during the hypnosis process in hope of getting them to act or respond in certain way. Most people are familiar with the hypnosis from the shows they've seen on stage. It is often used as a means of improving health too.

Peer Pressure-We all have an intrinsic need to belonging. This might be with a specific group, their families, acquaintances, and the community. With peer pressure tactics, the therapist works to suppress the doubts of the subject. Moreover, he works to help minimize the subject's resistance to new ideas by exploiting this strong need to belonging. If done correctly, the subject might be more willing to try new things, be less shy about new people, and make new friends easily.

Love Bombing-the sense of family in people is very strong. This is the group in which you were raised, and which has been around for your entire life. They have a rather complete understanding of how you work and feel than anyone else, and those who lack this kind of relationship can find themselves lonely and unwanted. During love bombing, through the use of emotional bonding, feeling and sharing and physical contact, the agent can create a sense of family. It allows the agent and the subject to connect in a familial way. This makes it easier to function in the old identity for transition into the new identity.

Rejecting Old Values — as stated a bit earlier in this chapter, the agent works to convince the subject to reject all of its own values. This operation is intensified by intimidation, physical threat and other ways. At the end, the subject would abandon the values and beliefs they once held and start accepting the new lifestyle that the agent suggests to them.

Confusing Doctrine — there will be a motivation in this strategy to brainlessly accept the new identity while denouncing any rationale the subject may have.

The agent achieves this by going through a complex set of lectures on a doctrine which will be incomprehensible. Through this phase the subject will learn to blindly trust what the agent is saying. This applies to both the doctrine or about the new identity that is being created.

Metacommunication —this technique is used when the agent attempts to inject subliminal messages into the subject's mind. This will be achieved when certain words or phrases that are crucial to the new identity are emphasized by the agent These phrases and key words are implanted into confounding long lectures which the subject will be made to sit through.

No Privacy — privacy is a right that will be lost by many subjects until they have migrated to the new identity that is being suggested to them. Not only is this eliminated as a way to make the subject's guilt and misconduct more evident, but it also removes whatever opportunity the subject has to objectively assess the facts that are being stated. If the subject is entitled to have privacy, they will have time to privately analyze the information given to them, and may feel that it is misleading or does not hold up to what they already believe. Taking away this privacy means the agent or agents are always around and the subject is being easily guided to the new identity.

Disinhibition–the agent urges the subject to offer childlike obedience during this technique. It makes the agent's job less complex in influencing the subject's mind.

Unbending Rules— the rules that the agent puts in place are often stringent and will never alter. Such rules are meant to make it difficult for the subject to think and act on its own; then, they'll spend their time doing just what the agent tells them to do. There are many different rules that might fit into this category, such as the rules that will be followed for the cycle of disorientation and regression all the way to how the subject is permitted to use medications, take breaks for the bathroom and meals. These rules are put in place to control the subject fully during the process of brainwashing. Verbal abuse— verbal abuse is one of the techniques used during the process of breaking down. Often, when bombarded with violent and foul language all the time, the subject will become desensitized. Physical abuse can at times complement or substitute verbal abuse.

Sleep deprivation —when a person doesn't get the amount of sleep they need they often become vulnerable and disoriented. This can help create the ideal environment the agent is searching for during the breaking down and confession stages of brainwashing. Moreover, the subject will be needed to do excessive physical and mental exercises in addition to the insufficient sleep in order to accelerate the process even further.

Dress codes— the implementation of a dress code further eliminates any flexibility the subject may have, as well as the option they are used like picking out their own clothes. Also, the subject will be required to wear the dress code followed by the rest of the group during the brainwashing process.

Chanting— the agent must work to remove any non-cult ideas which might be present in the subject's mind. One way to achieve this is by singing or repetition of the phrases used by those who follow the new identity.

Confession — confession is greatly encouraged in those who are transforming into the new identity from their old identity. During this process the subject must annihilate their own individual ego by confessing to the agent about their doubts and weaknesses. If they can let go of these issues, there can be the creation of the new identity.

Financial commitment— there will be financial contributions that must be met in some situations. This can be of some support for the agent. First, the financial commitment causes the subject to become more dependent on the group as the subject may be getting rid of past connections and associations. They will donate various assets in the hope that they will be able to overcome their shame and guilt. The asset could be their car, home, money or some sort of other financial contribution. They get connected financially with the new identity. The agent will also be able to take advantage of these financial contributions to further their own needs.

Pointing the finger — you'll feel a sense of righteousness when you can point your finger at someone else.

This is your way to tell the world that you are good just by pointing out some of the world's flaws. The agent may point out all the violence, bigotry and greed in the world before comparing it with the goods of the new identity to which the subject is being guided.

Isolation — if you're detached from all that's around you, it's hard to get external options and opinions that could change your mind. This is what the agent should aim for, because they don't want all their work to go down the drain. Those who are brainwashed will be isolated from society, friends, family, and any other logical influences that would affect their thinking.

Controlled approval— the agent must work to keep the subject confused and vulnerable during the breaking down phase. This can be achieved through controlled approval. The agent will punish and reward similar actions in exchange. This makes it difficult for the subject to know what is right and what is wrong.

Change in diet — adjusting the amount of food that the subject is permitted to consume is another technique used to establish disorientation while increasing the subject's propensity to emotional excitement.

When the agent drastically reduces the amount of food the subject is allowed to consume, they deprive the subject's nervous system of the nutrients needed to thrive. It is possible to add medications to the mix in this group.

Games— games are sometimes used to cause greater group dependency. Usually the games with obscure or hidden rules will be introduced that will not be understood by the subject. In some cases, the subject won't be told the rules and they'll have to work them out or the rules will change constantly. This technique allows for more control of the agent.

No Questions— the subject is not allowed to ask questions during the brainwashing process.

Questions encourage individual thinking which is harmful to the practice of brainwashing.

When no questions are permitted, this will help the agent gain an automatic acceptance from the subject to the new identity. Guilt— the subject was told that they had been bad, and that all they do is bad. Guilt is a common tactic the agent uses to challenge the subject's beliefs and whatever is happening around them. The sins of the former lifestyle of the subject will be emphasized to bring about the remorse and increase the need for salvation within the subject.

Fear — fear is a powerful motivator and can do much more than the other strategies mentioned above. Agents may use fear to maintain the desired obedience and loyalty within the group. To do this, the agent may threaten the subject's limb, heart, or soul for anything that is against the newly presented identity.

We will touch upon few techniques that can be used during the process of brainwashing. Each of them has the point of instilling the belief that the subject's old identity is false, and convincing them that the new identity is preferable.

There are many different ways this can be done, and when used as a combination, many will be more successful.

Although brainwashing can alter someone's way of thinking and behaving, most experts believe real brainwashing is exaggerated and cannot be achieved. While there may be few signs of brainwashing in everyday life, most people will not consider that this mechanism has altered their entire belief systems.

Chapter 5: Effectively Analyzing And Influencing People

Power and influence are closely linked, and influence is the product of the exertion of power.

5.1 Types of Influence

We can classify Influence into two major categories; Covert Influence and Overt Influence.

Covert Influence

In this type, both you and the individual being affected are conscious that the two of you are playing with certain powers. Essentially, this means everybody's cards are on the table, and everyone knows what everyone else is "holding."

Examples of this would be when some kind of trade is taking place, whether it be business or otherwise. Something like flirting would be a sort of covert manipulation, if we take a more personal approach, as you both know what is going on.

Overt Influence

This sort of influence is quite fascinating as you are aware of what is happening, but it is not the people that are being influenced. This type of influence usually revolves around changing the ecosystem, which is the relationship between humans, or people and their environment in this case. This form of power, however, is either frequently overlooked or exploited by leaders but can also have a significant impact.

Influencing the Ecosystem

Behaviors and attitudes have long been known to occur within an area, which in turn affects the people within it. The following three conditions are the most prevalent within an organization that can be changed.

Physical

Often, the easiest thing you can do is shape the climate to influence the ecosystem. It's important to remember that any physical changes you make can affect the organization's culture.

Noise

This can affect people's performance in the environment, either in a good or in a bad way. You'll often see in stores, for example, that they tend to play more upbeat music in an attempt to make you shop and buy more, as you're energized by it.

Variety

We all know that variety cracks through the monotony that sometimes creeps into our lives. It also leads to improved performance, and trying to change things for your team is a good idea as they will not only learn and grow from it but will also feel uplifted.

Seating patterns

The manner in which seating is set up in an organization has a direct influence on the people's interaction within it. If you want to stimulate conversation, then it is easier to have an open-plan office. If the option is to restrict this contact, however, since you want people to focus on their jobs, this will be done by placing people in "silos." "Silos" involves not only partitions between desks and the like, but putting teams on multiple floors or even buildings. **Psychological**

 The next thing you can do is focus more on the human side.

Small groups

You will often find that it is easier to manage and work with smaller groups and to guide them towards a particular goal.

Realistic expectations

If you have realistic goals but, at the same time, are slightly daunting for a person, you can find that they are motivated by the goals they set for themselves, as well as by a morale booster.

Increased contact

Increasing interaction with people will lead to increased feelings towards each other, either good or bad, depending on the person's present state. The most common example of that is trying to get people on certain days to go for lunch together. What you are trying to do at the end of the day is building relationships within the team.

Participation

Usually, if you increase a person's participation, they tend to feel more respected and, in turn, seek to be more successful in their work. The advantage here is that it can be extended to all workers, which in turn increases the overall productivity and performance quality and makes the sum of the parts more significant than the whole.

Magnetism

Magnetism is an invisible force that causes an effect of pulling as a result of a greater force. The force would be personal power in terms of organizations. Often you can wonder why some people listen to a particular person even if their status does not warrant that. These are the people you need to keep an eye on in the organization, as they are the ones who can influence people. Such people are very good at making things proliferate so you can use them to do that. There is nothing wrong with this if it is used for legitimate purposes, as you acknowledge, in an organization, that they are the catalysts or "change agents."

Sometimes this subject can sound very sinister when you manipulate people and situations, but it can be used for good or evil as with everything in life.

5.2 Covert Influence to Trigger Impulse

Most often, covert influence occurs naturally. And that's a shame because the effect of "normal" is similar to random and typically leads to unforeseeable outcomes that we later wonder what went wrong.

It can happen with the most significant decisions you can make in your life. Research published in May details the significance of what people look at while making a big decision.

The same moment we are making moral decisions, our opinions are affected by what our eyes are focusing on. Lund University researchers and other institutions have managed to influence people's responses to questions like "Is murder defensible?"by monitoring their eye movements.

When the participants had long enough seen a randomly pre-selected response, they were asked for an immediate response.

The response was chosen as their moral position by 58%.

The study shows that when we make the decision, our moral judgments can be affected by what we look at. Using a new experimental approach, the researchers monitored the eye movements of the participants and asked for an answer when their eye rested upon a randomly pre-selected response.

Covert Control involves the powerful hidden points of persuasion that form actions and attitudes. Covert Control is humanly regarded as the most important "tool" of persuasive communication "resources." Let's take one example.

The Trend of the Reward Card

These are the kinds of cards, restaurants, and other retail companies use to hold you as a customer by rewarding you for your loyalty. A lot of different places do use them, and when used correctly, they are powerful marketing devices. If one little thing is lacking, they are worthless.

What's unfortunate is that people think, "When didn't work for us," because they didn't understand the only way the card could be successful was what happened. They had an electronic tool but did not know how to turn it on. The Trend of the Reward Card is a shocking example of Hidden Control at work.

Covert Influence transcends bashing people over the head, arguing, battling, and almost all influence is felt on an unconscious level... For you... it's about understanding precisely what response another person will have to different stimuli in the world or with you.

Optimizing Covert Influence

Now let's see how to maximize your use of Covert Influence so you don't find yourself wondering why you lost after-sale business. This will also help you find out what went wrong with your well-conceived marketing strategy.

It's essential to have a list, set, structure, whatever you want to call it... a few hundred of these totally unknown causes, stimuli, behaviors at the tips of your fingers.

What really influences people (and often on!) off the written page are not so many phrases or vocabulary habits that are usually impotent.

What triggers the tumblers to transform in the brains of people is a multitude of reactions to different stimuli that all converge here and now.

Marketers at University are not hearing about it, because the material is not in textbooks for marketing. Therapists do not know about this in their books, perhaps because it is not in their textbooks. Instead, what you're studying here comes from a different world.... from cognitive neuropsychology, behavioral science, behavioral economics, decisionmaking, social psychology, and many other places that no one stops and looks at.

The "reasons" people say "no" or "yes" or "I'll think about it" become crystal clear when you start learning about Covert Influence.

5.3 The Most Subtle of Subtle

Let us explain it with an example. You take a trip you would not want to go on, but you wanted one more trip with your airline in order to qualify for your annual Platinum elite status. That status is beneficial over the course of the year, and it's worth taking a few days off and changing around your schedule to get those "qualification miles." Your option is NOT to have Platinum elite status, which can COST you many benefits you are enjoying.

The critical point is that you're traveling thousands of air miles, and if I stop you short of getting to the next certification stage, you will miss out on a lot of cool things.

Write it down. Bury that in your bones when people invest a lot in something they want to get what they believe is theirs.

You don't want your prize, victory, something you have earned, and any probable future benefit, no matter how small, to be lost or snatched or taken away because of any reason. We are possessive creatures. We possess objects, emotions, ideas, feelings, and even individuals.

If we've invested in a partnership or a product or service, or an idea, or a program, or a strategy, or stock, and "it's going down," then we'd like to be even.

Loyalty

You get coffee at Starbucks, stop at McDonald's for an Egg McMuffin, buy Morton Salt, purchase an iPod... for one reason.

It is the brand with which you do business. And a brand is about trust, and that creates loyalty. Loyalty has always played a very critical role in every business or family success. "THE REASON" people keep buying from you every now and then.... or not.

All the loyalty programs capitalize on various rules of Covert Influence in a very subtle manner. What is fundamental is that people want to be influenced

Saying "yes" to someone feels good, in contrast to saying "no" to somebody. Think about that.... because you don't have complaints when you buy, maybe you need an explanation, but not much more.

The reward program of the airline is not meant to save your money but rather to make your life simpler and more relaxed.

Suppose I am a loyal customer with a high loyalty rating. So, how do you convince me to switch on to some other company or brand? How do you capture and influence the perceptions of another company's loyal customers?

Because I'm loyal, it'll take a LOT to make me switch, but there's a threshold where I'll switch. Hence there is a threshold where EVERYONE will change. The key to bringing about that change lies in the manner the information is presented to the prospective client. It is only after then the quality and quantity of information assume importance. Recent research shows that the truly loyal individual would look for shortcomings in the goods of the competitors... to prove that this is not a good brand.

This is much easier to comprehend in the context of religion or politics.

If you're a loyal Democrat and someone asks you to switch your loyalties towards the Republicans, you're quick to point out the Republicans ' ideology flaws, thus revealing the Republicans' inferior standing.

You are searching for and seeking evidence to show that non-Baptist, non-Democrats, are bad, and your religious or political brand is excellent. So, when it comes to loyalty, the human brain thinks that way.

Key Point: In the end, the less loyal customer, relative, spouse views the brand of the rival as essentially the same as the brand being already used.

Through shifting the focus from differences to similarities, and vice versa, you can gradually shift the perspective of these very different life perspectives.

Key Point: It's not about tackling or overcoming objections to get people to buy you when they're loyal to X. Instead, it's about drawing parallels and similarities in your dissemination of information and facts. .In less loyal people, you want to shift their tendency from similarities to differences.

Mostly they are NOT loyal because they don't see any significant differences. Present evidence, so that glaring differences between A and B become instantly noticeable. .Only then you can make him switch to brand or product of your choice.

5.4 Secret of getting people to do a better job for you

15 Radiologists read scans of 318 patients at ShaareZedek Medical Center in Jerusalem. The CT scans were performed in color.

Upon opening the patient's computer file, the colored scans appeared immediately.

The focus of the study wasn't on the issue for which the scans were taken.

The emphasis was on accidental material. They were looking for a kidney cyst in patients through scanning.

When images of patients... of their faces... were included with the CT scans, the doctors found that 81 of 318 had incidental problems.

90 days later, all 81 of THOSE scans were once again shown to the physicians.

This time in 80 percent of those scans, the doctors found nothing wrong with the patient.

Does that qualify for a "wow? Covert Influence is terrifying, indeed.

With every doctor you meet, you can leave your photograph, and indeed... with every customer, you do business within general. A tiny 1 or 2'' tall/wide image is all that's required.

Influence without Resistance

You can master truly amazing strategies in predicting what and how your customer (spouse, kid, consumer, read: anyone) will choose. So, by applying the most critical trends in consumer research today, you can step ahead of anyone else.

Conclusion

Manipulation is an emotionally destructive psychological strategy employed by individuals who are unable to ask directly what they want and need, "says Sharie Stines, a therapist based in California who specializes in violence and toxic relationships. "People who try to influence others try to control others." There are many different forms of manipulation from a pushy salesperson to an emotionally abusive partner — and some actions are easier to spot than others.

According to Stines, fear, obligation and guilt Manipulative conduct includes three factors: fear, obligation and guilt. "When someone manipulates you, you're mentally compelled to do something that you really don't want to do," she says. You can feel scared to do so, motivated to do so, or guilty of not doing so.

She points to two common manipulators: "the bully" and "the victim." She says that a bully makes you feel afraid and could use violence, threats and intimidation to manipulate you. The perpetrator makes their target feel guilty. "Usually the victim is in the way of harm," Stine says. But while manipulators always play the victim, she adds that the fact is they're the ones that caused the problem. A person targeted by manipulators who play the victim sometimes tries to help the manipulator to stop feeling guilty, says Stines. Targets of this kind of abuse also feel responsible for helping the victim to end their pain by doing whatever they can.

Psychological manipulation It is a kind of social influence aimed at changing other people's behavior or attitude by indirect, misleading, or underhanded tactics. These strategies could be deemed exploitative and devious by promoting the manipulator's goals, often at the detriment of another.

It is not inherently a bad thing to have social influence. Individuals like friends, relatives and doctors, for example, may try to persuade people to alter obviously unhelpful attitudes and behaviors. In general, social control is viewed as innocuous if it respects the right of the affected individual to accept or reject it, and is not unduly intimidating. Social influence may constitute underhanded manipulation depending on the context and motivations. According to George K. Simon, a psychology author, effective psychological manipulation requires primarily the manipulator.

1.   Hiding belligerent intentions and behaviors and being affable.

2.   Understanding the victim's psychological weaknesses to assess which tactics would probably be the most successful.

3.   Have a sufficient level of ruthlessness to allow no reservations about harming the victim, if needed. Consequently, manipulation is likely to be done through covert offensive means. Weaknesses exploited by manipulators According to Braiker's, manipulators manipulate the following weaknesses (buttons) that may occur in victims:

•disease to please

• addiction to earning the approval and acceptance of others

• Emotophobia (fear of negative emotions; i.e., scared of expressing outrage, disapproval or frustration)

• Inability to say no and lack of assertiveness

• Blurry sense of identity (with fuzzy personal boundaries)

• Low self-confidence

• External locus of control.

According to Simon, manipulators manipulate the following weaknesses that may occur in victims:

- naïveté–victim finds it too difficult to accept the idea that some people are sly, devious and manipulative or are' in denial' if they are victimized.
- Over-conscientiousness–victim is too willing to give the benefit of the doubt to the manipulator and to see their side of things where they blame the victim.
- Low self-confidence–the individual has self-doubt, lacks confidence and assertiveness, and is likely to get too quickly on the defensive.
- Over-intellectualization–the victim tries too hard to understand, and assumes that the manipulator has some logical reason to hurt.
- Emotional vulnerability–the individual has a submissive disposition or dependence. The more the victim becomes emotionally dependent, the more vulnerable they are to abuse and manipulation. In general, manipulators take the time to map their victims ' attributes and vulnerabilities.

An expert on Psychology, Kantor advises: How Antisocial Personality Disorder affects all of us that susceptibility to psychopathic manipulators includes being:

too dependent–dependent people need to be accepted and are therefore gullible and prone to say yes to something they should say no

. • immature –has poor judgement and thus appears to believe excessive claims.

- Naïve–can't believe there are unethical people in the world, or take it for granted that they won't be allowed to prey on others.

- Easily Influenced-seduced by charmers. We might vote for, for example, the most charming candidate who kisses children.

- Confident–Honest people often assume that everyone else is honest. They are more likely to engage with people they barely know without verifying credentials, etc., and less likely to interrogate so-called experts.

- Carelessness not giving adequate thought or attention to damage or mistake.

- Solitary-lonely people can accept any human deal. A psychopathic stranger can offer human companionship against a price

- Narcissistic–narcissists are prone to fall for flattery without justification.

- Impulsive–for example, make snap decisions about what to buy or who to get married without consulting anyone.
- Altruistic-the psychopathic's opposite: too straightforward, too fair, too empathetic.

- Frugal–can't say no to a bargain, even when they know why it's so cheap.

- Materialistic-easy prey for loan sharks or fake getrich schemes.

- Greedy–greedy and dishonest fall prey to a psychopath who can easily persuade them to behave in an unethical manner;

- Masochistic –lack self-respect and thus unconsciously encourage psychopaths to manipulate them. They think they deserve it because of a sense of guilt.

- Elderly people–elderly people may become exhausted and less multi-task able. If they hear a sales pitch they are less likely to consider it a con. They are prone to giving money.

too dependent–dependent people need to be accepted and are therefore gullible and prone to say yes to something they should say no

Motivations of manipulators
There are many motivational factors that can influence manipulators to manipulate and control others, including:
- motivated to further their personal interests and gains at the cost of the other
- an extreme urge to gain feelings of superiority and power among others
- a desire to have control over things
- an urge to secure a sense of power over others so as to enhance self-esteem perception in the eyes of others
- monotony leading to lack of interest in the surroundings and seeking pleasure in giving harm to others

- hidden agenda which can be criminal like financial misappropriation meant to illegally capture the financial assets and funds of elderly or unsuspecting uber-rich people
- Not communicating with intrinsic emotions, phobia of commitment and subsequent rationalization (the perpetrator does not actively deceive, but instead tries to convince himself of the invalidity of his own feelings)
- Lack of self-control over impulsive and anti-social behavior, therefore pre-emptive or reactive manipulation to preserve the identity

Ways to Handle Manipulation

A person's reaction to manipulation is dependent on the kind and intensity of manipulation he is exposed to.

When you believe you, or someone you know, are in a coercive or even abusive relationship, experts suggest seeking support from or assistance from a therapist. A good support network, Stines says, can help too. "People in toxic relationships need to hear counterpoints. They're conditioned to believe that the interactions are natural. Somebody needs to help them break out of that misconception. "Stines advise that a person should not allow the manipulator or manipulative behavior to influence you personally. The best strategy should be to act as an observer and not as an absorber. After all: "We are not responsible for the feelings of anybody else." Also, setting boundaries will play an essential role in holding manipulation at bay. "Those who exploit have pitiful limits," says Stines. "As a human being, you have your own volitional experience, and you need to know where you end up and where the other person starts. Manipulators often have either too tight boundaries or too enmeshed boundaries. "According to Olson, it can also help delay your response in a manipulative situation. For starters, refrain from signing a contract, at first sight, do not make a large transaction without thinking through it, and the most important one is to desist from entering into major relationships in haste. Sleeping on it'" is often the only solution to avoid exploitation," continues Olson.

References

- "Definition of 'Manipulate'". www.merriamwebster.com. Retrieved 2019-02-24.
- Simon, George K (1996). In Sheep's Clothing: Understanding and Dealing with Manipulative People. ISBN 978-1-935166-30-6. (reference for the entire section)
- Braiker, Harriet B. (2004). Who's Pulling Your Strings ? How to Break The Cycle of Manipulation. ISBN 978-0-07-144672-3.
- Kantor, Martin (2006). The Psychopathology of Everyday Life: How Antisocial Personality Disorder Affects All of Us. ISBN 978-0-275-98798-5.
- Skeem, J. L.; Polaschek, D. L. L.; Patrick, C. J.;

Lilienfeld, S. O. (2011). "Psychopathic Personality: Bridging the Gap Between Scientific Evidence and Public Policy". Psychological Science in the Public Interest. **12** (3): 95–162. doi:10.1177/1529100611426706. PMID 26167886.

- Frank, Prabbal (2007). People Manipulation: A Positive Approach (2 ed.). New Delhi: Sterling Publishers Pvt. Ltd (published 2009). pp. 3–7. ISBN 978-81-207-4352-6. Retrieved 2019-11-09.
- Faggioni M & White M Organizational Psychopaths – Who Are They and How to Protect Your Organization from Them (2009)
- Baibak, P; Hare, R. D Snakes in Suits: When Psychopaths Go to Work (2007).
- Kernberg, O (1975). Borderline Conditions and Pathological Narcissism. New York: Jason Aronson. ISBN 978-0-87668-205-0.
- Aguirre, Blaise (2016). "Borderline Personality Disorder: From Stigma to Compassionate Care". Stigma and Prejudice. Current Clinical Psychiatry. Humana Press, Cham. pp. 133–143. doi:10.1007/978-3-319-27580-2 8. ISBN 9783319275789.
- Baron-Cohen, S (2012). The Science of Evil: On Empathy and the Origins of Cruelty. Basic Books. pp. 45–98. ISBN 978-0-465-03142-9.
- Casillas, A.; Clark, L.A.k (October 2002). "Dependency, impulsivity, and self-harm: traits hypothesized to underlie the association between cluster B personality and substance use disorders". Journal of Personality Disorders. **16**

(5): 424–36. doi:10.1521/pedi.16.5.424.22124. PMID 12489309.

- Kernberg, O. (1993). Severe Personality Disorders: Psychotherapeutic Strategies (New ed.). Yale University Press. pp. 15–18. ISBN 9780-300-05349-4.

- "On Manipulation with the Borderline Personality". ToddlerTime Network. Retrieved 28 December 2014.

- American Psychiatric Association 2000

- "Histrionic Personality Disorder". The Cleveland Clinic. Retrieved 23 November 2011.

- Christie, R., and F. L. Geis. (1970) "How devious are you? Take the Machiavelli test to find out." Journal of Management in Engineering 15.4: 17.

Dark psychology, mind control and Manipulation secrets

Learn the art of mind control, persuasion, emotional influence, brainwashing and hypnotherapy

By Michael Goleman

is the solitary and utter responsibility of the recipient reader. Under no circumstances will any legal responsibility or blame be held against the publisher for any reparation, damages, or monetary loss due to the information herein, either directly or indirectly.

Respective authors own all copyrights not held by the publisher.

The information herein is offered for informational purposes solely, and is universal as so. The presentation of the information is without contract or any type of guarantee assurance.

The trademarks that are used are without any consent, and the publication of the trademark is without permission or backing by the trademark owner. All trademarks and brands within this book are for clarifying purposes only and are the owned by the owners themselves, not affiliated with this document.

Chapter 1: Introduction To Dark Psychology Traits

Narcissism, egoism, Machiavellianism, psychopathy, sadism, spitefulness, and others are among the characteristics that stand for human personality's malevolent, dark sides. These characteristics share a common' dark core' as shown by the findings of a recently published German-Danish research project. Therefore, if you have one of those traits, you would possibly have one or more of the others as well.

Both world history and daily life are full of examples where people exhibit ruthless, malicious, or egotistical behavior. In everyday language and psychology too, we have various names to define the specific dark urges that human beings may have, most specifically psychopathy (lack of empathy), narcissism (excessive self-absorption), and Machiavellianism (with the core belief that the ends justify the means), the so-called' dark triad' and other traits such as egoism, sadism, or spitefulness.

"The Dark Triad" refers to what is regarded and perceived by many criminologists and psychologists as a simple indicator of criminal behavior as well as complicated, broken ties.

Dark Psychology Triad

Narcissism, Egotism, grandiosity, and lack of empathy

Machiavellianism

Uses deceit to manipulate and exploit people and has no sense of morality

Psychopathy

Sometimes charming and polite but marked by impulsiveness, selfishness, lack of empathy and guilt

We do not want to be exploited but end up being exploited one way or the other. We may not be exposed to the Dark Triad directly, but on a daily basis we face dark psychology tactics.

These tactics are often used in advertisements, web ads, sales techniques, and even the practices of our bosses. If you have children (especially teenagers) you will most likely experience these strategies. This is because the kids experiment with behaviors to get what they want and try to attain autonomy for themselves. In fact, the people you trust and love also use covert manipulation and dark persuasion tactics to achieve their goals. Here are some of the techniques that are common and are used by people most frequently.

Love Flooding

Compliments, affection or buttering someone to make a request

Lying

Exaggeration, untruths, partial truths, misleading stories

Love Denial

Withhold attention and affection

Withdrawal

Avoiding the individual or silent treatment

Choice restriction

Giving other options that divert someone from the option you don't want someone to make

Semantic Manipulation

Using terms that are meant to have a shared or mutual definition, but then the manipulator discloses that he or she has a different sense of the understanding of the conversation.

This book is written with the objective of creating awareness among people and to remind everyone how easy it is to use these strategies to get what we want. First, you should evaluate your tactics in all aspects of life, including your work, leadership, romantic relationships, parenting, and friendships.

While some people who use dark tactics know exactly what they do and are willing to manipulate you to get what they want, others are using dark and immoral tactics without being fully aware of it. Many of these people learned tactics from their parents during their childhood. Others learned the techniques in their teenage years or adulthood. They unwittingly used a manipulative tactic, and it worked. They got what they wanted. And they keep using tactics to help them get their way.

People are trained in some situations to use those techniques. Usually, sales or marketing programs use training programs that teach dark, unethical psychological, and persuasion techniques. Marketing programs use dark tactics to create a brand or sell a product solely for the purpose of serving their or company interests and not that of the customer. Most of these training programs assure people that there is nothing wrong with using these tactics and that they are meant for the overall good of the buyer. Consequently, as customers buy the product or service, their lives will be much easier.

Dark Psychology Users

Who uses Dark Psychology and Methods of Manipulation? Given below is a list of people who seem to make the maximum use of these tactics.

Narcissists

People who are genuinely narcissistic have an inflated sense of self-worth. They need others to substantiate their belief that they are superior. They've dreamed of being adored and worshipped. To maintain and sustain their beliefs, they use tactics of dark psychology, manipulation, and unethical persuasion.

Sociopaths

These are charming, intelligent, and impulsive individuals, yet they are genuinely sociopaths (meeting psychiatric diagnoses). They use dark tactics to build up a superficial relationship and then take advantage of people because of a lack of emotional feels and the inability to feel guilt.

Attorneys

Many lawyers concentrate on winning their case so intensely that they turn to using dark manipulation techniques to get the outcome they want.

Politicians

Some politicians use dark psychological tactics and dark persuasion tactics to persuade voters they're the candidates of their choice and thus succeed in winning their votes.

Sales People

Most salespeople get so obsessed with securing a deal that they use dark tactics to inspire and convince anyone to buy their product.

Leaders

Many leaders use dark tactics to ensure compliance from their subordinates and make them work with more significant commitment.

Public Speakers

Many speakers use dark tactics to heighten the audience's emotional state, realizing it leads to the drawing of the desired response.

Selfish people

These are persons who are merely interested in forwarding and achieving their personal interests with ulterior motives. First, they will use tactics to meet their own desires, even at the detriment of someone else. They don't mind win-lose results.

So, what's the difference between questionable psychological tactics and techniques of legal influence and persuasion? Some of the people fully agree that they often use these methods or that their companies need them to use dark practices as part of the company's processes for attracting and retaining clients.

This is truly unfortunate, and while contributing to short-term sales and revenue, it will ultimately lead to distrust, poor business practices, poor employee engagement, and less successful business results over the longer term.

To distinguish between those dark strategies of motivation and persuasion and those ethical, it is necessary to determine your purpose. We have to ask ourselves whether the tactics we are using intend to help the other person? It's all right for if these tactics do help you as well, but if it's just for your gain, you can easily fall into dark, unethical practices.

The goal should be to have a mutually beneficial result, or "win - win" situation. But you have to be frank with yourself and your assumption that the other person will really benefit. An example of this is a salesperson who assumes that everyone will benefit from his product, and because of the purchase, life will be a lot better for the consumer. A salesperson with this attitude will quickly fall into using dark techniques to get the person to buy his product and end up using a mentality of "end justifies the mean."

Do you want your leadership, relationships, parenting, work, and other areas of life to be truly successful?

Then evaluate yourself to decide your current motivation and persuasion tactics. Doing it right gives prestige and power in the long term. Doing it wrong (going dark) leads to weak character, broken relationships, and long-term disappointment as people will eventually see through the darkness and know your purpose.

The book will examine various types of dark psychology techniques and the most widely used deception techniques.

- Love Flooding
- Love Denial
- Manipulative Affirmation
- Exhaustion Manipulation
- Subliminal Control
- Preference Limitation
- Reverse Psychology
- Mind Games
- Brainwashing

While there tend to be significant discrepancies between such characteristics at first sight — although it might seem more 'acceptable' to be selfish than psychopathic — recent research indicates that all dark facets of human personality are various. That is, most dark characteristics can be interpreted as flavored manifestations of one specific underlying disposition: the dark center of personality. For a fact, this means that if you tend to show one of these dark features of your personality, you are also more likely to have a strong tendency to show one or more of the others.

As the new research shows, the common denominator of all dark traits, the D-factor, can be characterized as the general tendency to maximize one's individual usefulness— disregarding, embracing, or malevolently causing disutility to others— accompanied by beliefs that serve as justifications.

In other words, all the dark characteristics can be traced back to the general propensity of putting one's own goals and interests over those of others even to the point of taking pleasure in harming others— along with a host of convictions that serve as justifications and thus avoid feelings of guilt, shame, or the like. Evidence suggests that dark characteristics may usually be interpreted as instances of this common core — although they can vary in which aspects predominate (e.g., the aspect of justification is very high in narcissism, while the aspect of malevolently causing disutility is the main trait in the manifestation of sadistic behavior).

University of Copenhagen's Professor of Psychology, Ingo Zettler, along with his two German colleagues, Ulm University's Morten Moshagen and Koblenz-Landau University's Benjamin E. Hilbig, have shown how this common denominator is present in nine of the most widely studied dark personality traits:

- **Egoism:** There is an inordinate desire for securing personal gains neglecting the benefits and goods of other members of the other people
- **Machiavellianism:** It is marked by a display of callous behavior, manipulative skills along with the inspiration from "ends justify the means."
- **Moral Detachment:** Cognitive processing style that allows behaving unethically without feeling distressed
- **Narcissism:** Marked by an extreme need for public attention, self-conceit, self-praise, and feeling of superiority over others
- **Psychological entitlement:** One thinks that he is better and superior to others, so he needs to be treated accordingly and in a befitting manner

- **Psychopathy:** People display impulsiveness with poor empathy and inability to control personal actions and behavior
- **Sadism:** People seek pleasure or look for their benefit by inflicting physical or mental harm on the other party
- **Self-interest:** People are preoccupied with maximization of their personal, social and financial stature
- **Spitefulness:** People willing to indulge in self-harm in pursuit of the destruction of the other party

The researchers, in a series of studies involving more than 2,500 individuals, posed a question to the participants looking for their agreement or otherwise disagreement carrying the following statements:

- It is extremely difficult to make your way without hurting others' interests.
- There is nothing wrong with undergoing a little self-harm to ensure deserving punishment to others.
- I firmly believe that there is something special about me as the same is being told and ensured to me by others.

Besides, they studied other self-reported tendencies and behaviors such as aggression or impulsivity and objective measures of selfish and unethical behavior.

The researchers ' mapping of the popular D-factor, which has just been published in the academic journal Psychological Review, can be linked with how Charles Spearman found about 100 years ago that people who score high in one kind of intelligence test usually often score highly in other types of intelligence tests because there is something like a general intelligence factor.

Accordingly, the dark aspects of human personality also have a common denominator, which means that one can assume— close to intellect— that they are all a manifestation of the same inclination towards disposition," explains Ingo Zettler.

For example, the D-factor can often manifest itself in a given person as narcissism, psychopathy, or any other trait. It can also manifest as a blend of two dark traits. But by mapping the common denominator of the different dark personality traits, one can decide that the individual has a high D-factor. This is because he says the D-factor shows how likely a person is to participate in actions related to one or more of these dark traits. In practice, this means that a person who displays a specific malevolent behavior (like bullying others) will also have a higher likelihood of engaging in other malevolent behaviors, namely lying, stealing, or cheating.

The nine dark traits cannot be categorized as having identical potential, and each can contribute to certain typical types of behavior. The dark traits, however, usually have much more in common at their core, which in turn sets them apart. And information about this' dark core' can play a crucial role for researchers or clinicians working with people with particular dark personality traits since it is this D-factor that affects various kinds of careless and malicious human behavior and actions, frequently reported in the media.

We see it, for example, in corporate or public sector cases of extreme abuse, or rule-breaking, deceit, and deception. Knowledge of the D-factor of an individual can be a useful tool here, for example, to determine the risk that the person will re-offend or indulge in more harmful behavior, he says.

Chapter 2: Vulnerabilities, Traits And Motivations Leading To Manipulation

According to Braiker, the following vulnerabilities are exploited by the manipulators in their targets:

- excessive inclination to please others
- craving and weakness to earn the acceptance and the approval of people
- intense and unwarranted fear of vomiting, fear of undue expression of anger or frustration
- inability to stay no and lack of assertiveness
- blurry sense of identity (with soft personal boundaries)
- low self-reliance and external locus of control

Simon says that manipulators exploit the following vulnerabilities that may exist in victims:

Naïveté

It is very difficult for the victims to concur with the concept that people are ruthless, cunning and devious or is "in denial" if they are being victimized.

Over-Conscientiousness

Victim has increasing propensity to conceive the manipulator as innocent person and not ready to accuse him of any wrong doing

Low Self-Confidence

Victim has very little or low self-confidence, does not believe in his skills, suffers from low self-esteem and lack of assertiveness and is always employs a defensive approach

Over-Intellectualization

Victim has very poor analytical and assessment skills and generally finds a reason to justify the harmful actions of the manipulator

Emotional Dependency

Victim usually acts in a subdued and submissive manner and has a dependent personality. The emotional dependency of the victim leads to their vulnerability to exploitation and manipulation by the manipulator

Manipulators generally take the time to analyze and work out the victim's personality traits and vulnerabilities.

The author of the book, The Psychopathology of Everyday Life, illustrates how Antisocial Personality Disorder affects all of us and that this vulnerability enables psychopathic manipulators to achieve their goals because of following traits:

Dependent

These persons need to be loved. Hence they are, therefore, gullible and liable to say yes to something to which they should say no.

Immature

An immature has impaired judgment and so tends to believe exaggerated advertising claims.

Naïve

Such a person finds it hard to accept that this world is full of dishonest people. Additionally, he believes that if there are dishonest people in the world then their dishonest actions will be checked and countered and hence they will not be able to use others for their benefit.

Impressionable

These are easy to be tricked and used by charmers. For instance, they will get quickly impressed by a politician if they would see him kissing kids.

Trusting

Honest people that other people are also honest. They have the tendency to trust strangers without gathering desired information about them and hence will quickly commit their finances or other precious items to them.

Carelessness

These are people who do not give sufficient amount of thought or attention on harm or errors.

Lonely

These are very vulnerable and prone to accept any sort of guised noble act which is offered by a psychopathic stranger at any price.

Narcissistic

Narcissists have disposition towards flattery and thus can be easily targeted.

Impulsive

These are persons who make snap decisions about, for example, what to buy or whom to marry without consulting others.

Altruistic

They are opposite of psychopathic: too honest, too fair, too empathetic.

Frugal

They cannot say no to a bargain even if they know the reason it is so cheap.

Materialistic

These are easy prey for loan sharks or get-rich-quick schemes.

Greedy

These are the greedy and dishonest people. They can easily fall prey to a psychopath who can easily entice them to act in an immoral way.

Masochistic

They have no self-respect. They unconsciously allow psychopaths to use them to their advantage. Their sense of guilt makes them think that they deserve this kind of treatment.

Elderly People

The elderly people get fatigued easily. They are also not good at multi-tasking because of their age. They will not consider or construe a sales pitch as a con. Anybody with a hard-luck story can become a recipient of their money.

Motivations of Manipulators

Psychological manipulation is a type of social control aimed at changing the attitude or actions of others through techniques of underhandedness, deceit, or even violence.

By advancing only the manipulator's desires, often at the detriment of the other, these tactics could be perceived as exploitative, coercive, devious, and misleading.

Social influence does not necessarily have a negative effect. For instance, doctors seek to persuade patients to change unhealthy habits. Social influence is harmless because it respects and is not unduly coercive, the right of the affected to accept or reject it.

Social influence may constitute underhanded manipulation, depending on the context and motivations.

Manipulators may have different possible motives, including but not limited to the need to pursue their own interests and personal gain at almost any expense to others, and a clear need to achieve control and superiority feelings in their relationships with other people.

- An urge and desire to be in control of things
- A desire to attain a sense of power over others so that it can result in their self-esteem enhancement
- Feeling of boredom
- Getting tired of their environment
- A hidden agenda or plan which could be criminal and involves financial embezzlement(mostly the unsuspecting, unprotected wealthy, elderly or

unsuspecting people are manipulated for snatching the victim's assets)

- Suffer from lack of self-control over impulsive and anti-social behavior thus pre-emptive or reactionary manipulation to maintain image

Requirements for successful manipulation

Simon says that psychological manipulation can be successful if:

- Aggressive intentions and behaviors are concealed by the manipulator
- The psychological vulnerabilities of the victim are known to the manipulator enabling him to select the best effective tactics for successful manipulation
- The manipulator does not care about causing harm to the victim and has a severe sense of ruthlessness
- As a result, it could be referred to as covert manipulation (relational aggressive or passive-aggressive).

2.1 How Manipulators Control Their Victims

Braiker described the following basic ways which manipulators can use to control their victims:

Positive Reinforcement

Includes praise, superficial charm, superficial compassion (crocodile tears), an excessive apology; money, acceptance, gifts; affection, public recognition, a forced laugh or smile.

Negative Reinforcement

Includes nagging, yelling,

Partial or Intermittent Positive Reinforcement

It may motivate the addict to continue-the gambler is likely to win now and again in most forms of gambling, for example, but still lose money overall.

Punishment

This involves traumatic one-trial learning-using verbal abuse, violent rage, or other threatening actions to establish dominance or superiority; even an instance of such conduct may teach or train victims to avoid upsetting, challenging, or contradicting the manipulator.

Simon described the following manipulative techniques:

Lying

It's hard to tell if someone lies at the moment they do it, although often later when it's too late, the facts may become evident. In order to minimize the chances of being lied to, one has to realize that certain types of personality (particularly psychopaths) are experts in the art of lying and cheating, sometimes doing so in a subtle manner.

Lying by Intention

It is regarded as a very subtle form of lying, which uses concealing of a considerable amount of the facts. They also use this technique in propaganda.

Denial

Manipulator refuses to admit that something had been done wrong by him or her.

Rationalization

An explanation for inappropriate behavior is made by the manipulator. Rationalization relates closely to spin.

Minimization

This is a form of denial coupled with rationalization. The manipulator argues that his or her conduct is not as harmful or reckless as was implied by someone else, for instance, stating that a taunt or provocation was just for fun.

Selective Inattention or Selective Attention

During this process, the manipulator refuses to pay attention to anything that distracts from his agenda, saying, "I don't want to hear it."

Diversion

Manipulator avoids giving a straight answer to a straight question and moves the discussion onto another subject.

Evasion

It is similar to avoidance but involves giving meaningless, ambiguous, and rambling answers.

Covert Manipulation

Using veiled (subtle, explicit, or implied) threats to force the target onto the defensive.

Guilt-tripping

It's an intimidation technique of a different kind. A manipulator usually tells the conscientious victim that they don't care enough, are too selfish. It often leads them to feel bad, putting them in a position of self-doubt, insecurity, and submissiveness.

Shaming

Manipulator uses sarcasm and put-downs to heighten the victim's anxiety and self-doubt. Manipulators use this technique to make others feel undignified and therefore defer to them. Shaming tactics, such as a stern look or smile, offensive tone of voice, sarcastic remarks, overt sarcasm, can be very subtle. Manipulators can cause one to feel ashamed for even challenging them. It is an effective way for the victim to build a sense of inadequacy.

Playing the part of the victim

Manipulator presents him or herself as a victim of circumstances or actions of someone else in order to obtain compassion, sympathy, or elicit affection and thereby receive something from someone else.

Caring

Caring people can't stand to see someone hurt, and the manipulator also finds it easy to get help by capitalizing on the sympathetic nature of the victim.

Vilifying the victim

This technique is an effective way to put the victim on the defensive while simultaneously masking the manipulator's violent intent.

Playing the servant Role

Cloaking a self-serving agenda in the form of serving a nobler cause, for instance, claiming he is behaving in some way for "obedience" and "service" to God or a similar figure of authority.

Seduction

Manipulator uses charm, praise, flattery, or openly supporting others to make them lower their defenses and make them give their confidence and loyalty to him or her.

Projecting the blame (blaming others)

The manipulator scapegoats in ways that are often subtle, hard to detect during this phase.

Feigning innocence

Manipulator tries to say that any harm done was accidental or did not accuse them of doing something. Manipulator pretends to be outraged or surprised by such an act. This strategy calls the victim into questioning their own judgment and probably their own sanity.

Feigning ignorance

Manipulator tries to play naive by pretending that he or she doesn't know what you're talking about or is puzzled about a significant issue brought to his attention.

Brandishing anger

Manipulator brandishes sufficient emotional intensity of anger and rage to scare the victim into submission. In reality, the manipulator is not angry; instead, he or she puts on an act. He only wants what he wants, and when denied, is "angry."

Psychological Characteristics of Manipulators

Persons with any of the following psychological conditions can be classified as Manipulators:

Machiavellian Personality

This is a little-known personality disorder in contrast to psychopathy and narcissism. People who have this personality disorder are usually unemotional. They tend to manipulate and deceive people on a regular basis and frequently.

They typically agree with statements mentioned as under:

1. Without hurting others or their interests, you cannot advance further.

2. You must not disclose the reason for any of your actions until and unless you see some benefit in doing so.

3. People have hidden agendas and plan which will get exposed only at the right time.

4. Flattering privileged class is right for achieving objectives.

These traits are named after the 15th-century Italian diplomat. The people with these traits are experts in getting others to do what they want. They achieve this by lying and flattery.

If they had one, their slogan would be: "The ends justify the means." This means that you can indulge in any sort of activity to achieve a favorable result.

They understand what motivates other people, and exhibit cold selfishness to get something from. Despite this, they are so good at manipulating that others who do not know their evil intentions often like them much.

One of the so-called' dark triad' of malevolent personality types is the Machiavellian personality.

Experts on dark personalities, Drs Daniel N. Jones and Delroy L. Paulhus, explain: "They were so-called because individuals with those characteristics have a propensity to be callous, arrogant and malevolent in their interpersonal dealings."

Psychopaths and narcissists are familiar to most of the people, but very few have heard of the Machiavellian! The temperament of the Machiavellian people tends to be nasty and undependable, causing them to lie, steal, and betray when it benefits them.

In comparison to the psychopath, the Machiavellian keeps a close eye on his reputation.

Narcissistic Personality Disorder

Narcissistic Personality Disorder is a disease in which the individual feels superior, has superficial feelings, displays little-no empathy, and has a grandiose sense of self.

DSM-IV separates personality disorders into three clusters based on similarities between the symptoms:

- Group A people are typically schizotypal, schizoid, paranoid with the odd or eccentric disorders

- Group B consists of histrionic, borderline, narcissistic, antisocial people with the erratic, emotional or dramatic issues

- Group C people are obsessive-compulsive, dependent, avoidant and suffer disorders of anxiousness and fearfulness

Traits of People with NPD

People suffering from NPD must exhibit any five of the following characteristics.

1. Lacks empathy
2. Has the belief that he or she is "special" and unique and can only be understood by other special people
3. Does not hesitate to take advantage of others to achieve his or her own ends
4. Usually has an exaggerated feeling of importance over others
5. Lives in a fantasy world dreaming of unlimited success, power, brilliance, beauty, or ideal love
6. Requires excessive admiration
7. Strong sense of entitlement
8. Thinks that others envy him or jealous of him
9. Arrogant affect

Borderline Personality Disorder

The borderline personality disorder (BPD) is a personality disorder characterized by extreme "black and white" thinking, mood swings, emotional dysregulation, disturbed relationships. People with this disorder have problems and difficulty in functioning in a way society accepts as normal. The name comes from the DSM-IV-TR; the ICD-10 has an equivalent called Emotionally Unstable Personality Disorder, borderline type. Psychiatrists describe borderline personality disorder as a severe disorder characterized by pervasive instability in the mood. Lack of stability in behavior, interpersonal relationships, and self-image are also some of the symptoms of this disorder. Consequently, this instability often disrupts family and work life, long-term planning, and the individual's sense of self-identity.

Originally thought to be at the "borderline" between psychosis and neurosis, people with BPD actually suffer from what has come to be called emotional dysregulation. While less well known than schizophrenia or bipolar disorder (manic-depression), BPD is more common among young adult women as two percent of them are suffering from this disorder. Although the people do not exhibit suicidal intention in this disorder, however, they have a high rate of self-injury. However, in severe cases, there have been significant cases of suicide attempts. In some instances, people with BPD kill themselves by accident in the case of self-injury that goes too far. Usually, the patients need extensive mental health services, and they account for 20 percent of psychiatric hospitalizations. With help, however, many improve over time and are eventually able to lead productive lives.

Traits of People with BPD

People with BPD may exhibit the following personality traits:

1. Intense and extreme efforts to avoid real or imagined abandonment.

2. Exhibit unstable and intense interpersonal relationships characterized by alternating between extremes of idealization and devaluation

3. Identity disturbance: markedly and persistently lowly view of personality

4. Increased impulsivity in at least two areas that are potentially self-damaging (e.g., spending, sex, substance abuse, reckless driving, binge eating;

5. Repetitive suicidal behavior, gestures, or threats, or self-mutilating behavior

6. marked mood reactivity like irritability, anxiety, or intense episodic dysphoria

7. Severe emptiness feelings

8. Inordinate anger or difficulty controlling anger (e.g., frequent displays of temper, constant anger, recurrent physical fights)

9. Severe dissociative symptoms, transient, stress-related paranoid ideation

Dependent Personality Disorder

Dependent personality disorder (DPD), formerly known as an *asthenic personality disorder*, is a personality disorder that is characterized by a pervasive psychological dependence on other people. The difference between a 'dependent personality' and a 'dependent personality disorder' is somewhat subjective, which makes diagnosis sensitive to cultural influences such as gender role expectations.

Traits of People with DPD

People with DPD may exhibit the following personality traits:

1. Find it challenging to make everyday decisions independently and dependent on advice and reassurance of others for his decision-making

2. Not willing to assume responsibility for personal actions and decisions

3. Find it difficult to express disagreement with others because of fear of loss of support or approval (this does not include realistic fears of retribution)

4. Lacks self-confidence, fearful of consequences, doubts personal abilities and skills and thus finds it challenging to take up or initiate new projects

5. Not shy or hesitant of doing unpleasant things in search of gaining support and assurance of others

6. Extremely uncomfortable or helpless when alone because of exaggerated fears of being unable to care for himself or herself

7. Urgently seeks another relationship as a source of care and support when a close relationship ends

8. Is unrealistically preoccupied with fears of being left to take care of himself or herself

Histrionic Personality Disorder

This is a personality disorder that begins in early adulthood and which involves a pattern of excessive emotional expression and attention-seeking, including an extreme need for approval and inappropriate seductiveness.

The salient symptom of the histrionic personality disorder is the display of attention-seeking behavior marked by a pervasive and excessive pattern of emotionality. Individuals suffering from this disorder are usually enthusiastic, flirtatious, and lively. The individuals can be sexually provocative, express strong emotions with an impressionistic style, and be easily influenced by others.

Traits of People with HPD

People with HPD may exhibit the following personality traits:

1. Constant seeking of reassurance or approval
2. Excessive dramatics with exaggerated displays of emotions
3. Extreme sensitivity to criticism or disapproval
4. Inappropriately seductive appearance or behavior
5. An utmost concern with physical appearance
6. An urge for securing the attention of everyone
7. Extremely low tolerance for frustration or delayed gratification

8. Rapidly shifting emotional states that may appear shallow to others
9. Opinions are easily influenced by other people, but difficult to back up with details
10.   Make rash decisions
11.   Speak dramatically but with few details and facts to back up opinions
12.   May exaggerate physical illness or injury for attention

Passive-Aggressive Behavior

Passive-aggressive behavior refers to passive, sometimes obstructionist resistance in interpersonal or organizational circumstances to authoritative orders.

A means of dealing with stress or anger, it sometimes results in the person attacking other people in explicit, subtle, and often passive ways. It may manifest itself in the performance of requested tasks as anger, stubbornness, procrastination, sullenness, or deliberate failure. For instance, somebody who is passive-aggressive can take so long to get ready for a party they don't want to attend, that the party is almost over when they arrive.

Some people are more inclined to generate this behavior than others, and it can sometimes be considered a personality trait. When this type of behavior becomes so severe and omnipresent that it produces an ongoing, self-perpetuating psychological degree of disturbance in people's daily lives and interpersonal relationships, it can be called a passive-aggressive disorder of personality.

Someone who is passive-aggressive will usually not directly confront others about issues but instead will attempt to undermine their trust or success through comments and actions that, if questioned, can be innocently explained away so as not to blame the passive-aggressive person.

2.2 Traits of People with Passive-Aggressive Behavior

People with this disorder may exhibit the following personality traits:

1. Ambiguity

2. Avoiding responsibility by claiming forgetfulness

3. Blaming others

4. Chronic lateness and forgetfulness

5. Complaining

6. Does not express hostility or anger openly

7. Fear of competition

8. Fear of dependency

9. Fears authority

10. Fosters chaos

11. Intentional inefficiency

12. Making excuses and lying

13. Obstructionism

14. Procrastination

15. Resentment

16. Resists suggestions from others

17. Sarcasm

18. Sullenness

Type A Angry Personalities

The Type A personality is also known as the Type A Behavior Pattern. It is a collection of characteristics that includes being anxious, overly time-conscious, insecure about one's position, highly competitive, hostile, and violent, and unable to relax. Type A individuals also extreme workaholics who multi-task, drive on with deadlines, and are frustrated about the slightest delays. They have been identified as stress junkies, and often show some of the following features:

1.   An underlying insecurity or absence of self-esteem, which is considered the root cause of the syndrome. It is assumed that this is covert, and thus less observable.

2.   The urgency of time and impatience, causing frustration and exasperation.

3.   Free-floating animosity that can be triggered in the face of even minor incidents.

Antisocial personality disorder

Antisocial personality disorder (APD or ASPD) is a psychiatric diagnosis describing antisocial and impulsive behaviors as signs of a personality disorder. Professional psychiatry typically compares APD to sociopathy (not to be confused with psychosis) and psychopathic disorders. Statistics show that every 3 of 100 men 1 of 100 women are thought to have some form of DSM-IV antisocial personality disorder.

Traits of People with APD

It is characterized as a persistent pattern of disrespect for and violation of the rights of others that have occurred since age 15. People with this condition are expected to demonstrate any of the following three characteristics:

1.   Failure to comply with social norms about lawful behavior as demonstrated by repeatedly performing acts which are grounds for arrest

2.   Deception, as demonstrated by frequent deception, the use of aliases, or conning others for personal gain or enjoyment

3.   Impulsiveness or a failure to plan ahead

4.   Repeated physical fights or assaults suggesting irritability and aggressiveness.

5. Reckless disregard for self-safety or safety of others

6.   Consistent irresponsibility, as shown by repeated failure to maintain steady work or to fulfill financial obligations

7.   Lack of remorse, as indicated by being indifferent to or rationalizing the damage, maltreatment or theft of others

Chapter 3: Mind Control-Techniques

Mind control, also known as brainwashing, reeducation, brain-sweeping, coercive persuasion, thought control, or thought reform, is a general term for a number of theories that suggest that the thinking, actions, emotions, or decisions of a person that, to a greater or lesser extent, can be arbitrarily manipulated by external sources. Some quotes related to mind control are given below:

Donald Ewen Cameron: Life is For Living as quoted by Harvey Weinstein in Mother, Son, and CIA. 100.

If we can succeed in inventing ways to change their attitudes and beliefs, we will find ourselves in possession of strategies that, if used wisely, could be used to liberate ourselves from their attitudes and beliefs in other fields that have contributed significantly to the volatility of our time by their unwillingness to keep up the progress.

Noam Chomsky, Deterring Democracy (1992), p. 357

Thought control is more necessary for independent and popular regimes than for the despotic and military states. The rationale is straightforward: a despotic state may violently control its domestic enemies, but as the state loses this weapon, it requires new devices to prevent the ignorant masses from interfering in public affairs that may not be of their concern.

CIA interdepartmental memo Project ARTICHOKE January 1952

Can we get hold of a person to the degree that he bids against his will and even against fundamental laws of nature, such as self-preservation?

Edward Hunter on Brainwashing, New York: Pyramid Books p. 185-186

Brainwashing is a system that allows a person to be seduced into embracing what would otherwise be abhorrent to him. He loses touch with reality. Facts and fantasy whirl around and change places... But to prevent people from understanding the intrinsic evils of brainwashing, the Reds say it's just another term for something already very familiar and of unquestioned importance, like education or reform.

Stephen A. Kent (1997) Brainwashing

Social scientists need not change their concept of brainwashing, but should simply acknowledge that brainwashing is used by at least one contemporary political group in an attempt to retain its members While this research cannot address critical questions about the long-term consequences for people who have been through this specific brainwashing method (compare Schein, 1961: 284), there is no denying that the founder of Scientology has given considerable thought to the practices of brainwashing and imposed them on those of his members who he felt were harboring feelings or taking action against him or her. Therefore, the word "brainwashing" has validity within some debate in the social sciences.

B.A. A. Robinson (1996) Glossary of religious and spiritual terms

Brainwashing is (thought control, mind control, coercive persuasion) a non-violent method that uses mind control techniques to convince a person to abandon some of their fundamental beliefs and adopt the beliefs of the indoctrinator.

Margaret Singer (1997)-Cults in Our Midst

In this book, she says that a significant number of political, religious, and economic groups are operating in the U.S. alone. The number of their members has reached the figure of an astounding 2.5 million. Cults, over the last ten years, have used tactics of coercive mind control to negatively impact an estimated 20 million victims in the previous ten years. Worldwide figures are even more significant.

Benjamin Zablocki (2002)

Benjamin Zablocki defined it as a process by which individual or collective freedom of choice and action is compromised by agents or agencies that modify or distort perception, motivation, affect, cognition, and behavioral outcomes. It is neither magical nor mystical, but a process that involves a set of basic social psychological principles. ... It seems to me that at the very heart of the controversy over the existence of mind control is a bias toward believing in the power of people to resist the power of situational forces, a belief in personal will power and faith to overcome all evil adversity. It is Jesus modeling resistance against the temptations of Satan and not the vulnerability of Adam and Eve to deception. More recently, examples abound that challenge this person-power misattribution.

Abusive Power and Control

It is also referred to as the technique of controlling behavior or coercive control. It is the process in which the prime goal of securing power, maintaining, and controlling power is to make others a victim of financial, sexual, psychological, or physical abuse. There can be various motivational factors for the said purpose. These could be envy, personal gratification, devaluation, psychological projection, or personal gain. All this is done for enjoyment gained from establishing control and power over others.

Abusers make use of techniques to exert power and control over their victims. The methods themselves are physically and psychologically violent at times. Control may be aided by economic exploitation, thus restricting the actions of the victim as they may then lack the resources required to combat the violence. The abuser's goal is to control and threaten the victim or to force the victim to believe they have no equal voice in the relationship. Manipulators and abusers manipulate their victims with a range of strategies including positive reinforcement (e.g., encouragement, superficial charm, flattery, ingratiation, love bombing, smiling, gifts, attention), negative reinforcement, intermittent or partial reinforcement, psychological manipulation (e.g., nagging, silent treatment, cursing, threats, bullying, emotional blackmail, and guilt trips. The victim's vulnerabilities are manipulated, with those especially vulnerable being most commonly chosen as targets. Traumatic bonding may occur between the offender and the victim as a result of repeated cycles of violence in which the periodic strengthening of reward and punishment produces powerful emotional attachments that are resistant to change and a climate of fear. There may be an attempt to normalize, legitimize, rationalize, dismiss or diminish the abusive behavior or blame the victim for it. Many frequently used tactics include isolation, lying, disinformation, propaganda, destabilization, brainwashing, and divide, and rule. To disorient them further, the victim may be plucked with alcohol or drugs or deprived of sleep. Many types of personalities feel especially compelled to dominate others.

Control Freaks

Control freaks are often perfectionists who protect themselves against their own inner vulnerabilities with the belief that they risk exposing themselves to childhood trauma once again if they are not in total control. These individuals exploit and force others to change so that they do not have to improve themselves and use control over others to avoid an inner void. When the cycle of a control freak is disrupted, the controller is left with an awful sense of powerlessness, but feeling their pain and fear brings them back to themselves. Control freaks have the traits of Type A personality in terms of the personality-type theory, motivated by the need to dominate and control. It also correlates an obsessive need to monitor others with an antisocial personality disorder.

Psychological manipulation

Braiker described the following ways that manipulators manipulate their victims:

Positive reinforcement

This involves praise, superficial charm, superficial compassion (crocodile tears), excessive apology, money, acceptance, gifts, publicity, facial expressions such as a forced laugh or smile, and public recognition.

Negative Reinforcement

This involves removing one from a negative situation as a reward, e.g., "If you allow me to do this for you, you won't have to do your homework."

Intermittent or partial reinforcement

Partial or intermittent negative reinforcement may build an efficient climate of fear and doubt. Partial or occasional positive reinforcement may inspire the victim to proceed.

Punishment

It involves nagging, yelling, silent treatment, bullying, threats, cursing, emotional blackmail, guilt trip, sulking, weeping, and the victim playing.

Traumatic one-trial learning

In this technique, the manipulator uses verbal abuse, explosive rage, or other threatening actions to establish dominance or superiority; only one incident of such conduct can condition or train victims to avoid upsetting, challenging, or contradicting the manipulator.

Emotional blackmail

Emotional coercion is a term coined by psychotherapist Susan Forward, about controlling people in relationships and the idea that fear, responsibility, and guilt (FOG) are the transactional dynamics at play between the controller and the individual being controlled. Understanding these mechanisms is helpful for anyone struggling to get out of another person's controlling behavior and coping with their compulsions to do things that are unpleasant, unwelcome, burdensome, or generous to others. Forward and Frazier each describe four forms of coercion with their own style of mental manipulation.

Form 1: Punisher's Threat

The manipulator, for example, could force you to eat the food he's prepared, or harm you.

Form 2: Self-Punisher's Threat

The manipulator, for example, can force you to eat the cooked food, or it may harm himself.

Form 3: The Sufferer's Threat

For example, the manipulator could force the food to cook by claiming he's saved it for himself and has no idea what he can do with it after your rejection.

Form 4: Threat from the Tantalizer

The manipulator could instigate you to eat the food by offering ice cream as a reward.

Silent treatment

Sometimes silent treatment is used as a control mechanism. When used in this manner, it represents a passive-aggressive action characterized by the combination of nonverbal but nonetheless unambiguous signals of the presence of negative emotions with the refusal to discuss the scenario that causes those emotions and, where the cause of those emotions is unknown to the other party, sometimes the unwillingness to explain or even to identify the source. As a result, the silent treatment perpetrator refuses the victim both the opportunity to negotiate an after-the-fact resolution of the claim in question and the right to alter his / her potential actions to avoid further offense. For particularly difficult situations, even if the victim gives in and accedes to the initial demands of the perpetrator, the perpetrator may continue the silent treatment to ignore the victim's input that suggests that those demands have been met. The silent treatment thus enables the perpetrator to cause harm, to get continued attention in the form of repeated attempts by the victim to restore communication, to retain a position of power by generating confusion over how long the verbal silence and related difficulty of resolution will last, and to obtain the gratification that the perpetrator correlates with each of these consequences.

Mind games

One definition of mind games is a mostly conscious battle for strategic one-upmanship, often using passive-aggressive behavior to demoralize or disempower the target of thought directly, making the aggressor look superior, commonly referred to as "power games."

In intimate relationships, mental games can be used to undermine the trust of one person in the validity of their own perceptions. Personal experience may be denied and pushed out of memory. Such manipulative mental games can extend to denying the reality of the victim's social undermining and trivializing what is considered necessary. Both sexes are equally vulnerable to such verbal abuse, which may unintentionally be carried out as a result of the need to preserve one's own self-deception.

Divide and Conquer

A primary strategy that the narcissist uses to assert control is to create divisions between individuals, particularly within their families. This helps the abuser in weakening and isolating them, making it easier for him to manipulate and conquer. Some are preferred, some are treated as scapegoats. In a workplace setting, these dynamics will work out.

The "wheel" of power and control was created in 1982 by the Minneapolis Domestic Abuse Initiative to clarify the essence of abuse, delineate the methods of abuse used to manipulate another person, and inform people to prevent violence and abuse. Power and control regarding aggressive physical and sexual abuse are usually present.

The abusers are often initially attentive, charming, and caring, gaining the trust of the person who will ultimately become the victim, commonly known as the survivor. The abusers are excessively interested in the emotions, thoughts, and actions of their partner when there is a bond and a degree of trust. Next, they set small rules and show "pathological jealousy. The cycle of conditioning usually starts with caring alternation, followed by abusive behavior. According to

Counseling Survivors of Domestic Abuse, "These serve to confuse the survivor contributing to powerful conditioning mechanisms that influence the self-structure and cognitive schemes of the survivor." The abuser projects blame for the violence on the victim or survivor, and the denigration and derogatory expectations are integrated into the self-image of the survivor.

The consequence of repeated cycles of violence is traumatic bonding, in which the intermittent reinforcement of reward and punishment produces powerful emotional attachments that are resistant to change.

Power and Control in Violent Relationships

Abusers use several tactics to exert control and influence over their partners. According to Jill Cory and Karen McAndless-Davis, writers of When Love Hurts: A Woman's Guide to Knowing Violence in Relationships: Each of the strategies within the power and control wheel is used to "maintain power and control in the relationship. No matter what techniques your partner uses, the purpose is to manipulate and threaten you or to force you to believe you don't have an equal voice. The victim may face threats that they will be returned to welfare, injured, or reported. The abuser might be trying to commit suicide. They may also compel them to act unlawfully or drop charges against the abuser that they may have. Strangulation is a severe type of coercive control, an especially pernicious abusive activity in which the abuser literally has the victim's life in his hands. Sorenson and others have called strangulation the waterboarding equivalent to domestic violence, which is widely regarded as a form of torture.

The abuser generates intimidation and fear through unpredictable and inconsistent behavior. One of four types of sadists may seek absolute control: explosive enforceable, brutal, or spineless sadists. The victims are at risk of anxiety, dissociation, depression, guilt, low self-esteem and suicidal thoughts.

Intimidation

Abused individuals can be threatened by brandishing weapons, damaging their properties or other things, or using gestures or looking to generate fear.

Threatening to use a weapon, for example, or merely showing the weapon, is a means of intimidation and coercive control.

Economic exploitation

Regulation of their access to money is an essential means of ensuring control and power over another. One strategy is to stop receiving or maintaining a work from the abuse. Abusers secure control on their access to money by withholding information and access to family income, taking their money, forcing the individual to ask for money, granting them an allowance, or filing an attorney's or conservator's office, especially in the case of elderly economic violence.

Emotional abuse

Emotional abuse involves calling by name, playing mind games, downplaying the victim, or humiliating the offender. The sole goal is to make the person feel bad about himself, feel guilty, or think they're mad.

Minimizing, denying and accusing

The abuser may deny that the abuse occurred and try to place the victim's blame for their behavior. Another part of this regulation is mitigating issues or the degree of violence.

Using children and pets

The abuser threatens to take the children or make them feel guilty about the children may use children to exert control. It might include bullying them during a visit or using the kids to relay messages. Another technique that controls is the abuse of pets.

Using privilege

Using "privilege" means the abuser determines the roles in the relationship, makes the critical decisions, treats the victim like a servant, and behaves as "the castle master."

Workplace manipulation

The power and control model built for the workplace has been categorized into the following categories:

- Overt acts
- Covert actions
- Emotional control
- Isolation
- Economic control
- Tactics
- Restriction
- Management privilege

Bullying

An underlying condition for bullying is the perception of a social or physical power imbalance for bullying to be executed.

Workplace Psychopaths

The writers of the book Snakes in Suits: When Psychopaths Go to Work outlines a five-phase model of how a typical workplace psychopath rises to and retains power:

Entry

A psychopath will commonly use highly developed social skills and charm to obtain employment in an organization. It will be difficult at this stage to spot anything that is indicative of psychopathic behavior. You, as a new employee, might perceive the psychopath as being helpful and even benevolent.

Assessment

A psychopath will analyze you and assess your usefulness. You may be regarded as either a pawn (who has some informal leverage and can be easily manipulated) or a patron (who has formal control and will be used by the psychopath to defend against attacks).

Manipulation

A psychopath will establish a "psychopathic fiction" scenario in which positive knowledge relating to psychopath and other negative aspects and attributes will be developed. This is the time when your role as a part of a network of pawns or patrons will be utilized, and you will be groomed into accepting the psychopath's agenda.

Confrontation

A psychopath will use character assassination tactics to uphold his / her agenda, and you will either be discarded as a pawn or used as a patron.

Ascension

This is the time when your role as a patron in the psychopath's quest for power will be dismissed, and the psychopath will take a position of power and prestige for himself from anyone who once helped them.

Institutional abuse

Institutional abuse is a person's mistreatment (often children or older adults) from a power system. This can vary from acts similar to domestic child abuse, such as neglect, physical and sexual abuse, and hunger, to the consequences of assistance programs operating below acceptable standards of quality, or relying on punitive or unjust ways to change behavior.

Human Trafficking

Effective coercion by perpetrators and traffickers requires the use of excessive control. High amounts of psychological stress caused by threats, fear, and physical and emotional violence are exposed to the victim. Coercion techniques are generally used in three phases of trafficking: recruitment, initiation, and indoctrination.

Traffickers use foot-in-the-door or intimidation tactics during the initiation process to direct their victims into various trafficking industries. This exploitation creates an environment in which the victim is wholly dependent upon the trafficker's authority. Traffickers use family dysfunction, homelessness, and childhood abuse records to exploit women and children psychologically into the trafficking industry.

A trafficker's aim is to turn a person into a slave. To do this, the perpetrators use tactics that can contribute to the psychological effect of the victims ' learned helplessness, where they believe they no longer have power or control over their lives. Traffickers can trap their victims, expose them to large amounts of alcohol or drug abuse, keep them in solitary confinement, or deny food or sleep. The patient also begins to feel the symptoms of depression, remorse and self-blame, anger and rage, and sleep disturbances, PTSD, numbing, and intense stress during this period. Under these pressures, the victim can fall into the mentally hopeless state of learned helplessness.

Children are particularly vulnerable because they are so young to these developmental and psychological consequences of the trafficking. Traffickers also harm the children's physical and mental health through repeated physical and emotional abuse in order to gain complete control of the child. Often, Stockholm syndrome is a common problem for girls while being trafficked, which can prevent them from both trying to escape and going forward in psychological rehabilitation programs.

Serial Killers

One form of serial killer's primary goal is to obtain and assert control over their victim. These killers as children may have been abused in their early life thus leaving them as adults with feelings of powerlessness and inadequacy. Many dominant or control-motivated killers sexually abuse their victims. Still, they differ from hedonistic killers in that rape isn't motivated by desire (as it would be with a lust murder) but merely as another means of victim domination.

Chapter 4: Covert Hypnosis

Covert hypnosis aims to communicate with another person's unconscious mind without informing the subject that he will be subjected to hypnosis. This process is also called conversational hypnosis or sleight of mouth. This term is mostly used by advocates of neuro-linguistic programming (NLP). NLP is a pseudoscientific approach to communication and interaction.

The technique's prime objective is to change the person's behavior subconsciously in such a way that the target believes that he changed his mind using his own will. The success of this process lies significantly in the fact that the remains unaware that he was hypnotized or that anything unusual occurred. There is, however, a debate as to what hypnosis is and how covert hypnosis should be classified. The focus and attention of the subject are imperative during the conduct of "Standard" hypnosis. On the contrary, covert hypnosis attempts to focus on "softening" the subject by using confusion, fatigue, directed attention, and interrupted sentences. This process is identical to salespeople talking to customers when they are tired. This is because critical thinking and questioning of statements require mental effort. The theme of "covert hypnosis" lies in approaching the subject when he is mentally and physically worn out. Covert hypnosis, irrespective of the fact, remains hypnosis. The element of fatigue is incorporated to make the critical thinking process more cumbersome. This explains why interrogation, military training, and cult-recruitment practices prefer to deprive their recruits of sleep.

4.1 Techniques

There is no significant difference between Covert hypnosis and indirect hypnosis, as derived from Milton H. Erickson and popularized as "The Milton Model in style. The notable trait of this process is that the hypnotized individual ultimately engages in hypnotic phenomena in an incognizant manner. There is a striking similarity between Covert hypnosis and "Ericksonian Hypnosis" in that both techniques work to reach deeper levels of consciousness operate by employing covert and subtle means . The surface structure of language then touches these more profound levels of consciousness. During covert hypnosis, the hypnotist controls another individual's behavior through establishing. The operator or hypnotist makes suggestions during the process of hypnosis while ensuring that the subject remains unaware of the suggestions being made.

The hypnotist builds rapport with the listener. At the same time, the hypnotist maintains psychological congruency (the act of genuinely moving to goal accomplishment without hesitation), both linguistically and in one's nonverbal communication. The subject feels a psychological connection with the hypnotist as he listens to him. The hypnotist, while displaying confidence and control, presents linguistic data in the form of metaphor:

The purpose of this metaphor is to offer a surface structure of meaning in the actual words of the story. This process then activates an associated deep structure of meaning that is indirectly relevant to the listener. However, it consequently helps in enabling a recovered deep structure of meaning that is directly relevant to the listener.

Put in another way, this process first builds unconscious states within the listener and then connects those states through covert conditioning. This process is also known as covert anchoring, which ultimately paves the way for the creation of unconsciously controlled behaviors and thoughts. The listener is tricked by making him believe that he is not the focus of the hypnotist's attention, and instead, the hypnotist is talking about something else. This is achieved, for instance, by shifting the use of time and use of identity in language.

An example

The hypnotist may try to achieve the state of forgetfulness in the subject. This is done when the hypnotist talks with the subject of his feeling in that particular state in order to gain maximum knowledge about the subject. When the hypnotist discovers that this state is at its heightened peak , he can start talking about that state after this state has attained its maximum peak. He can generally begin to by relating to a concept like the unsuspecting subject's name (a phenomenon called name amnesia). The typical result would be that the subject will suddenly be unaware of his/her name on questioning. That response will be contingent upon the fact that the suggestions were made to draw an immediate effect, and the reader was suggestible enough to be influenced in this way. The core objective of covert hypnosis is to shut down or at least minimize the analytical part of the subject's brain, lest he suspect something. All this may be achieved relatively quickly by an experienced practitioner.

Covert hypnosis and Media

Real estate expert Glenn Twiddle in June 2010 appeared on the Australian television show A Current Affair. The segment reveals how he teaches real estate agents how to use these tactics on potential property buyers.

Covert hypnosis in fiction

Covert hypnosis has been portrayed in television series such as The Mentalist, although somewhat over-represented, the most prominent portrayal of covert hypnosis was in the "Russet Potatoes" episode in which a suspect uses covert hypnosis to manipulate characters in the episode and attempts to kill her boss. Another example of covert hypnosis was in the X-Files, where a man with a tumor in his brain is learning additional hypnosis abilities and using it to escape police captivity.

Learning Covert Hypnosis

If you want to learn covert hypnosis, first, you have to realize that it takes a long time to master properly, but if you practice every day, you will continually see positive results.

When learning how to do covert hypnosis, the difficulty for most people is not their inability to apply the methods, but rather their impatience and ignorance of how covert hypnosis is first and foremost.

There are extremely useful tips given below that will help you learn covert hypnosis.

Get into the Right Learning Mind Frame

It involves understanding how it takes dedication and persistence to master covert hypnosis. When you start learning covert hypnosis first, do not think it's going to be easy.

Covert hypnosis is all about knowing how the human mind functions and discovering how to interact effectively, mentally, and physically, with someone's mind in a subtle way.

While you can learn and apply such methods effectively within a very short space of time, you will not be able to do this effectively to different people without understanding the full processes leading up to that point.

Build Rapport

Many people make mistakes while establishing rapport. Relationship building involves creating a secure connection between the hypnotist and the subject of the hypnotist. The stronger the bond, the more powerful the technique of covert hypnosis is.

The partnership is more than what exists out there. It is an emotional and intense friendship, where people can be inside the minds of each other.

This hypnotic relationship bond is so strong that the subject will see the hypnotist as a figure of authority, and will be more than willing to do what the hypnotist wants them to do with little or no resistance.

Look For Trance Signals

Widening the social awareness networks by increasing the senses is of fundamental importance. It is construed as a critical step as it helps you to see the signs the subject gives as they enter a hypnotic trance.

Recognizing sure trance signs ensures you can move to the next stage of your technique of covert hypnosis. Recognizing when someone is not hypnotically reacting to you is just as crucial because then you will realize that your manipulation is not working and that you have to find another process.

Understand Hypnotic Language

There is another name for Covert hypnosis, that is, conversational hypnosis, and you need to learn how to practice and sharpen your language skills to make it more hypnotic to influence a conversation.

Whenever you decide and manage to converse in a hypnotic language, it will cause the mind of the subject into a hypnotic state, which you can then influence to respond to in some hypnotic ways.

There is a range of primary and advanced methods in the hypnotic language, and you can do to achieve the hypnotic state of mind, from emotional triggers to manipulating someone's emotions to hypnotic storytelling.

4.2 What Hypnosis is and Hypnosis is not

It is essential that you clear from the outset any doubts you have about hypnosis. Hypnosis is presented in the media as a means of total control over another person, and this enormous misconception has affected many people.

Any form of hypnosis won't give anybody complete control over the mind of another. This is just not possible. Perhaps it is like a negotiation with the unconscious mind, the place where the values and ethics of an individual are stored.

In the case of hypnotism, you will never be able to get them to violate their firm beliefs, morals, and ethics, even if you happen to have reasonable control over someone's mind.

Advantages of Covert or Conversational Hypnosis

You are directly influenced by the level of happiness and success of the others. If you discover the fundamental secrets of ethical power, the world will be at your feet.

If you don't, you could end up living a quiet, lonely life, just like 95 percent of people who suffer from all kinds of problems needlessly.

Their suggestions and advice do not get much attention. They don't get their due respect. They lose clients and customers, and don't know why!

They are unable to communicate with confidence and have difficulty expressing their proposals to their colleagues. When they meet strangers, they lose their composure and make a poor initial impression.

They cannot get their children to listen and are usually discouraged because things don't seem to be going their way.

But it does get worse!

This is because no one tells you how to be as successful as you grow up. You've just picked up a few things here and there.

4.3 Covert hypnosis is a simple way to convince people

Another big problem is conventional communications, and it doesn't work out by mere sales training.

People are taught outdated methods, pushy and aggressive strategies, and complicated ideas in real-world situations which fall flat on their face. You'll see people run away from you if they find you using such techniques.

There's a plethora of proof to suggest hypnosis might just be the answer you've been waiting for. The best part is the right kind of trance, which even works every day during routine interactions. That's Okay. If you are talking to someone at a grocery store, at the post office, or elsewhere, you can successfully induce trance in them. Conversational hypnosis is the technical term for this type of hypnosis.

It is the most potent way of influencing the human mind positively. Over the past 65 years, scientific research has shown that hypnosis can be used in a secret manner. You can create ideas in the minds of people when communicating with them. They are not even going to know it's happening.

By learning to use covert hypnosis in an ethical way you can:

• Get what you want with ease so that life becomes a pleasure rather than a war!

• Enhance trust to communicate effectively in intimate, social, and professional environments!

• Grab the attention and admiration of people who are important to you!

• Quickly get others to agree with you without the usual stress and frustration!

Neuro-scientific experiments suggest that all learning behavior and change take place in an unconscious manner in the beginning. Afterward, the conscious mind catches up. So, if you want to be more successful, you've got to reach the people in their unconscious state. This is where the magic transpires. Hypnosis offers the fastest way to tap into the unconscious mind! Research in the field shows the secret to persuasion is not to try to change people's minds but to alter their attitudes first. For instance, you must first get somebody in the right mood. Only then can you change their perception and ability to agree with your point of view successfully.

Doctors, psychiatrists/psychiatrists, and hypnotherapists have found that: hypnosis opens the mind to suggestion to the point that "normal" mechanisms in the brain can be overridden. At the unconscious level, it works profoundly to create near-instant shifts in hypnotic subjects.

The problem is that regular hypnosis is not possible. You can't walk around, holding a pocket watch, asking people to "look deep into my eyes." Traditional forms of hypnosis are best suited to clinical circumstances. However, you absolutely cannot apply any sort of hypnosis in everyday interactions. If you tried, at best, you will look foolish and outrage people at worst. The conversational or implicit hypnosis is therefore suitable for typical situations. You can actually hypnotize someone who unintentionally asks for your assistance when chatting over a cup of coffee with them. Covert or conversational hypnosis:

- Is easy to learn, ethical to use and enjoyable when you perform every interaction
- Melts vital conscious mind resistance and makes way for easier and faster hypnosis
- Participants simply don't know they're being hypnotized
- Activates the suggestibility core of the brain so that thoughts sink into the unconscious mind and take root instantly

- Creates the atmosphere for bringing someone else in.

4.4 Research-Based Evidence on Use and Utility

Over 3,000 professional research papers conclude hypnosis is a proven way to initiate positive lasting change. Doctors and scientists around the world believe that hypnosis is an instrument that yields results. Since the early 1950s, the American Medical Association has allowed doctors to use hypnosis.

Covert Hypnosis Explained

Covert hypnosis can take many forms. It can be used as a pure and simple form of self-hypnosis, or it may be used to hypnotize another person or group of people.

Whether you choose to hypnotize yourself or another by using conversational hypnotism, the first step you'll want to take is to bring yourself in the desired state.

Getting Ready for Covert Hypnosis

You do not need to learn how to do hypnosis for yourself. Just relax by taking a few deep breaths in through your mouth and letting them out through your nose slowly and gently.

You don't need to do that in a way that's transparent to others. Whether standing or sitting, if you do it gently, it's pretty easy to do without drawing attention to yourself.

Allow your jaw and shoulders relax, and feel your hands softening across your arms. Let it flow down your torso, across your buttocks, through your legs and down to your toe's tips.

Be mindful one hand can feel warmer than the other. Feel the melting of your entire body, and as that fuzzy sensation slowly engulfs you, let your eyes smooth and become slightly hazy.

If someone else is talking to you when all of this is happening softly inside you, don't be shocked if he suddenly yawns; it's hard to do so without having any effect on anyone around. Once you're put in a territory, you'll find others sinking into it too.

No need for volunteers

You don't have to have a willing volunteer or participant to be an effective hypnotizer. Some people say they cannot be hypnotized, or they've never been hypnotized. We know that it is not so. Let them believe what they want.

It is true that hypnotizing someone who has been put on notice that he is about to be hypnotized and who purposely opposes the idea is very difficult-some may say impossible.

But a smart hypnotist does not make a note of an uncooperative or reluctant participant.

In reality, he doesn't even ask whether he wants to hypnotize the other. He is just going ahead and doing it in a much more subtle way.

Irresistible hypnosis

What you don't foresee you don't resist, and when you think hypnotism might have been used on you, it's pretty much too late, and it's all over by then.

Anyway, the person who is convinced that he cannot be hypnotized would afterward dismiss it as a flight of fancy and deny it ever took place. Why would the hypnotist worry about that?

Persuasiveness

We are all involved in day-to-day persuasion strategies to make something happen. We use some hypnotic methods to a greater or lesser degree anyway.

But the more you know about them, the higher your chance of achieving your desired outcomes.

Salespeople and Covert Hypnosis

We are all salesmen, no matter what we do. Professional salespeople learn to use weasel phrases and embedded commands in their sales pitches.

You may just be selling a point of view or an idea to colleagues at work, or be attempting to persuade your club committee.

It all amounts to the same thing, and for the same reason, specific strategies are available to you. If you do a regular analysis of them, you might be watching your performance rise a little faster than you had imagined.

Second, get into the state by calming yourself, and then watch the other person's body language very carefully. Be very careful not to imitate, but suit some of the more subtle body languages. If, while speaking, he leans forward, lean forward on occasions.

Endeavor to keep the eye contact and help the other get into the same place as you. Whether he is speaking quickly or slowly, he strives to match his tone and volume.

So slowly change your language pitch and speed so that he will follow you instinctively, and you will be able to control the conversation.

Dictate the pace with Covert Hypnosis

He will pursue you if you do so slowly and sympathetically. Now that you control the conversation's pace and tone, it's time to make your suggestions in the form of embedded commands or weasel words, perhaps.

The subtler you express your thoughts, the more likely it is that they will affect the unconscious mind of the other person.

Hypnosis Coaching Benefits

You can quickly see how valuable this method is if you are involved in life coaching or executive coaching or mentoring or guiding others. Once you have managed to get the person in the desired state, you can fill him with constructive feedback and motivation.

It's a shame that those strategies are not available to more students. By putting their pupils in the state and then using positive and encouraging orders and recommendations to improve their performance, they could produce even better results.

Luckily, there are many talented teachers among us, but some perpetuate the misconception that some pupils are "gifted" while others are not. Those who believe they are not in the category of "gifted" instead give up all too quickly.

If you're a trainer, you might want to consider adopting Conversational Hypnosis as best practice. If you do, you can watch the grades of your student's skyrocket, and your credibility as a teacher can soar as their success soars.

Anchoring Benefits

Learn about anchoring, too, as this is a reliable NLP technique, particularly useful in hypnosis. Suggestions can be strengthened by touching, for example, or analog marking by using pauses or emphasis in voice, or even by your stance or the position in which you sit or stand.

Story-telling and Covert Hypnotism

Maybe storytelling is the most potent form of persuasion in conversational hypnosis. A well-told tale has its own hypnotic influence as it allows the other person to go inside himself, take pictures, and look for meanings. In speaking, figure out what the beliefs of the other person are. Everybody has a different set of values.

What matters to me is not always what matters to you, and vice versa; neither is it wrong, but different. You will soon discover the beliefs of the other person by asking him to talk here and there, and giving him a verbal nudge. They will quickly emerge if their overarching values center family or sport, and you can tailor any story you use to express your compelling message about family or game as necessary.

Reliving the moments

The trick for coaches is to speak in a positive rather than pompous way before the game about past successes. He must concentrate on thrilling, match-turning moments.

You just had to look at the heads of the players to watch them relive the moments. By the time they're going to have to go on to the playing field, they're going to be in the arena, pumped up with positive advice and excitement, ready to take on their rivals.

Just precisely the same way, you can manipulate so many circumstances in your daily life to work for and not against you. Conversational hypnosis is a huge asset!

Covert Hypnotism and self-hypnotism

Conversational hypnosis is an excellent self-hypnotic process. You may be in a group of people who listen to someone who is an endless bore.

Using the chance to let his words take you to a different place where you can relax and focus on certain things that concern you.

Practiced well enough, if you have to participate later, you can still recover a few threads of his voice. After all, boring people just tend to repeat themselves!

Essential Skills for Becoming a Hypnotist

Imagine being the sort of conversational hypnotist who has been able to influence almost everybody you meet. So much so, you will inspire them to do great things with ease. Even an outdated mentality can change. But that is just the start.

You will take things a considerable distance further until you understand the methods and concepts involved so that people's faces light up with joy when you step into a room. So, when you ask your teenage kids to do something they accept without putting up the smallest amount of resistance. So, your customers want to do more business with you because they feel compelled to be in your company. Mastering secret hypnosis can make you irresistible.

You are going to ooze beauty effortlessly. You will gain the power to make every connection with others better, more meaningful, and much more straightforward. You can increase the ability to influence people by making sure they have more fun every time they're around. You're going to get people to do what you ask in a way that makes them feel good about it somehow. In other words, once you have the strategies and skills of covert hypnosis under your belt, you can make the world a better, happier, more exciting, and more desirable place to live.

4.5 The 3 Key Traits for a Hypnotist

Before you can unleash your abilities on the people around you, you need to bear in mind these three things:

1.   Know covert hypnosis is not just a knowledge collection. It is an emotional state. This is something of an attitude. If you want to do something using these abilities and accomplish something, then it is imperative that you approach it with the right mindset.

2.   Covert hypnosis makes use of tried and tested concepts of hypnosis to give extra strength and power to your thoughts and ideas. Once you put these concepts into action, all that you do and say will encourage you to communicate with the unconscious mind of the other person.

3.   It depends on your body language, vocabulary, and thoughts.

The three characteristics mentioned above will give you all you need to make life more enjoyable for yourself and everyone around you.

Let's break them down to see what is involved in each part of the process and the different strategies that come under each.

H+

You probably have heard about H+ or read about it. H+ refers to the willingness to communicate with others from the moment that the conversation starts. It's all about purpose, putting your thoughts and opinions aside so that you can get in touch with the person before you.

It is plus hypnosis. It is hypnosis with extra positive energy. Hypnosis tailored to doing all you can to make life more enjoyable and satisfying for the other person.

Going First

When you are hurt or in agony, then try to smile at someone even in this condition, or try to help someone relax when the thoughts of a stressful situation at work fill your mind.

It is challenging to handle such a precarious situation. There is too much incongruity between what you think and what you say and do.

In other words, if you keep conflicting ideas about it in your head, you can't work on one thing, because those contradictory ideas will show in your performance. In the way you speak, in the language of your body, your actions, the tonality of your voice, and even your breathing style. Hence before making or establishing any contact, you must try to get yourself into the right frame of mind.

Suppose someone you know, for example, is always feeling stressed. A few minutes with your hypnosis abilities, and they should feel much more comfortable, lighter, and happier like a weight lifted off their shoulders.

Establishing Report

How do you build a rapport?

Could you smile and shake hands in ordinary circumstances. You may be thinking about something that you have in common, like a particular sport or a hobby. You might have identical sharing of school or college experiences.

These are traditional ways of forming a partnership with someone else. And then, the bond is hypnotic. Recall that the purpose of each form of hypnosis is to connect with the unconscious mind of another person. This is where the magic takes place. So, when we're talking about a relationship in terms of hypnosis, it's a bit different.

Ever noticed how you find it incredibly convenient to start and maintain a conversation with some people? You seem to touch it, and never run out of words. Although keeping the conversational ball rolling with other people can be a mammoth task, like trying to climb up a hill when there's a fleet of monster trucks dragging you down.

Why is this happening? Because people are comfortable in their skin that you hit it off with. On an unconscious level, they are signaling to you that they feel good about themselves. They project a kind of confidence and security aura that helps you to open up and feel relaxed inside of yourself.

However, the others completely send out a separate set of messages. You know they're uncomfortable, anxious, hesitant, and probably scared to say the wrong thing. Or, they don't want to say anything. And that will make you feel uncomfortable and less willing to engage.

Needless to say, you want to be the same as the previous group. You want to express a sense of trust, a sense of tranquility, a sense of comfort, and security.

It's all tied to H+ and to going first.

The ABS Formula

You need to be able to achieve three things if you want to perform any kind of hypnosis on another human.

These three things that make up the ABS Formula are as follows:

A-Stands for Absorb Attention

Hypnosis is a natural state of mind that is highly focused. It is not based on what is happening in the outside world, but on what is happening in the unconscious mind inside.

That's why you've got to draw the other person in, drag them into the hypnotic experience, so you get their attention. Because let's face it, nothing you do will make the slightest impression on them if you have not got their attention.

And if you don't have their focus, how could you hope to put them into a trance?

It is not as hard to get somebody's attention as it sounds. You can do it easily by:

- Getting into their H+ state of mind
- Establishing eye contact
- By telling them a story, a metaphor or something they'll find interesting

- Hijacking something, they're thinking about and moving the conversation into something more hypnotic

Showing them an image or illustration can also be effective

B–Stands for Bypassing the Critical Factor

What does the critical factor denote?

This is part of the intellectual consciousness. It is the voice that analyzes everything in your mind, makes decisions, and rejects facts. If you find yourself saying, "I can't do that" or "That won't work," it's at work. It just fills the mind with a lot of limitations. Since the objective is to get to the unconscious mind, you must bypass the critical factor and stop interfering with it.

You need to avoid the other person from being frustrated so that they can push past those limitations and enjoy new and exciting experiences.

Several different strategies will encourage you to do that involves using:

- Engaging stories
- Power words and verbal bridges

- Hypnotic themes
- Hot words

S –Stands for Stimulating the Unconscious Mind

You should be aware of by now that where you are headed. Once you have the other person's attention, and have bypassed their critical factor, you have already begun to activate the unconscious mind. You have already started the process of getting them into a hypnotic state.

As you can imagine, it's a dynamic process. It can transpire or materialize within minutes, or even seconds. It's broken down into steps to give you some insight into what's going on, but it should be quick and flowing in reality.

All of the above-listed methods for bypassing the critical factor can be used in conjunction with each other. Let us take a look at each of these one by one.

Enchanting Subjects with Engaging Stories

Everyone loves a good story, whether they read it themselves, have it read to them, or watch it on a television. Stories have the ability to take us to locations and at different times. They permit us to stand out for some time from reality. They put on hold our everyday lives.

Stories can narrate anything that might have been experienced by you or something that happened to someone else like you heard or read about in the My Friend John style.

The other person starts listening as soon as you start telling a story. They want to learn more. They're keen to hear what's going on, who's doing what, how the storyline is unfolding, and how things end up getting resolved.

Even the most gripping story can become better by spicing it up. Metaphors and similes can be used to make them more powerful and engaging. So instead of saying that you had an enjoyable meal out, you might comment that your steak was as soft as butter. Maybe the restaurant was as posh as a palace, and you were treated as a royal by the serving personnel.

Using Power Words & Linguistic Bridges

One device is more powerful than all the others put together when it comes to hypnosis. You might even argue that it would be difficult to hypnotize without it. And that useful tool is words. In order to qualify as a hypnotist, you should have the skill and experience to use the words in the right context. Anybody can do it. Hypnotists use words and phrases specifically to help people imagine possibilities. It means they need to choose their words carefully. We call these words power words of choice (or hypnotic words of control). Power words are just nothing other than terms that you regularly use, whether you're answering the phone, talking to a neighbor, or talking to a friend about an idea. Once they hit a certain level, they're not hidden words. You don't need to be a grandmaster so that you can use them. These are not reserved for a lucky few who are fortunate after years of study to make use of them. What makes the words of influence are not just the words themselves but the way they are used. Hey! That's really the secret behind calling them "hypnotic words."

Words with Magical Power

How can well-known and frequently used words put a person in a trance? Let's look briefly at the character of words in general

Suppose someone asked you to imagine you biting yourself into a lemon. You can still do it without having a lemon in your mouth. You can feel eating within the yellow skin. Everywhere you can feel the juice squirting away and dripping. You can taste the sour citrus that nearly takes your teeth to the brim. You can even smell the lemony scent.

So, your saliva glands get stimulated somehow even without holding a lemon in your hand or biting it in.

That is what words are capable of doing. They are capable of:

- Stimulating your imagination
- Distracting you
- Painting pictures in your mind
- Activating your senses
- Making connections
- Linking two items that wouldn't usually go together

You've undoubtedly heard the phrase "cool as a cucumber"-but does it make any sense?

Cucumbers aren't particularly cool unless they are stored in the refrigerator. You can go to any garden plot and reach one, and you will find it is not colder.

4.6 The Big 5 Hypnotic Power Words

You can use thousands of power words. Let's continue with those words we call the Big 5.

1. Because

Example: "Since you're listening to me, you can relax, and because you're relaxing, you can feel comfortable because comfort produces more relaxation so you can relax even more comfortably and because you're relaxing right now, you can feel more comfort growing inside you."

2. And

Example: "You should relax and feel comfortable, and the relaxation that you think will make you relax even more, and the more ease you feel, the more relaxed you become. And you'll feel more comfortable as you relax. You'll relax more and more, as you feel more comfortable. For relaxation, it is essential to relax more and feels comfortable, so that you can relax and feel comfortable and relax even more and feel more comfortable.

3. As

Example: "Listening to my voice, you can start focusing your attention on the inside. As the concentration of your attention is inward, your unconscious mind begins to take you into a trance. You will feel an ever-deepening comfort starting to build as you breathe in and out.

4. Imagine

Example: "Imagine going into a trance? Imagine drifting on a steady rive on a sunny day. Imagine your muscles becoming loose and limp. Imagine yourself relaxed. "

5. Which

Example: "Since you have been studying these language patterns for some time now **which means** that you are learning something of tremendous value. The reason that you are reading this right now **means** that you are learning at the unconscious level...."

The examples mentioned above clearly demonstrate that the subtle and smart use of these words can unleash their power when they are used in a proper manner in the desired setting.

It is much easier for you as a hypnotist to put someone into a trance when they're relaxed. So, let's use the idea of relaxation to demonstrate how the power words might work. Given below are a few examples for your understanding:

"You realize that you can relax your body because you've been relaxing in the past." "And the more you relax, the more relaxed you become." "When you feel the relaxation running through your body, you know that each of your muscles can just let go and relax comfortably."

 "It is rather easier to picture yourself in a totally comfortable and happy position by spending more time on relaxing."

These power words serve their own purpose when used separately, but when they are used in combination, it gives a tremendous boost to their ultimate effect and overall power. By the way, at the beginning of this book, you might have found these same power words. If not, look right now and see if you can.

To hypnotists, words are especially useful because they have their hypnotic power. That is why so many parents often sing their babies to sleep with a lullaby, even in the 21st century. The words and rhythms have a consistency of soothing ness that nothing else can match.

10 Extra Power Words

You might have found that the Big 5 Hypnotic Power Words act as ties or linguistic bridges, seamlessly uniting ideas. It makes sense, therefore, that one of the simplest and easiest ways to start triggering a trance is simply to say: "Close your eyes and go into hypnosis." The word "and" ties the two ideas together, closing your eyes and going into hypnosis.

But as you know, to go into hypnosis, you need not close your eyes. But if you shut your eyes, you're not guaranteed to be going through hypnosis. Yet luckily, this is not open to your unconscious mind.

And as soon as you begin to think about what the words mean; you cannot help but begin to imagine the possibilities.

Since words in the mind can create connections and paint images, they are the fastest way of activating the unconscious.

And now, here are ten more power words (or phrases) to apply to your toolkit on hypnosis. Now let's look at some of these words and phrases in-depth and how to use them together.

Beginning with the "Just pretend" power phrase... Many people know how to pretend. It is something that you start to do in the first few years of life. But pretending does something magical. This permits you to turn your conscious mind off. To circumvent and let go of the critical factor, because that is what pretending is all about.

And you might say something like this: "Just imagine that you're at the most relaxing place you've ever been to. Only pretend that you are more confident than you used to be. Only try to slow down your breathing. "First, keep building the image in their head. "And the more you relax, the more you feel comfortable. You will feel more comfortable when your body will feel more relaxed. Due to the power of the words, you can use them in a whole host of different ways and still get fantastic results. Let's bring a few of them together in a short demonstration: "You can feel more and more comfortable each time you take a breath. To know what it's like when every muscle in your body is fully relaxed, free of tension. Just imagine that you were relaxing like that right now. "And with these words, literally, there is no limit to what you can achieve.

"Try to remember a time when you were so relaxed, so incredibly comfortable, and as you remember that feeling of total peace, imagine what it would be like if you could get that feeling back, right now, so you are in the deepest and quietest state of calm imaginable. So fresh that you know that you can really let go and unwind. The moment you feel overwhelmed by that feeling of serenity, you know you'll experience an excellent sense of relaxation sooner or later... "So, you see, using the definition of relaxation, all you're really doing is using together a few phrases. But they have a combined power when brought together that is almost sure to bring about the desired state and results.

Power Words Catalyze the ABS Formula

The justification for doing one of these things is clear: putting someone in a trance. You can only communicate with them when they're in a trance to either solve their problems or cope with their problems.

Of course, we are talking about a hypnotic induction. And as you probably already know, a specific formula follows a hypnotic induction.

We call that the ABS Formula. Let us briefly go through the three things you need to use to trigger a trance:

A: Absorb Focus

B: Bypassing the Critical Factor

S: Stimulating the Unconscious

In case you haven't noticed it yet, that's precisely what those hypnotic power words are designed to help you achieve: all three things at once.

As a kid listening to a lullaby, the clients will be swept away in the words and phrases you use, as well as by the repeated themes. We are not going to be able to stop themselves, because of course, the words and phrases are stimulating.

You win the focus of people by engaging them subtly. The inherent and built-in power of the words gives them an addictive consistency, allowing you to overcome the critical factor. And if, as a result of what you have said to them, they suddenly feel more comfortable, then that is an unconscious response.

They're not doing anything, after all, only listening to you, and yet their bodies respond positively to your suggestions. Not because they control it but because the information is transmitted to their unconscious mind.

And now, let's find out exactly how to put these words of power to work in a variety of different situations.

One thing you'll notice about the power words in the examples above is how they make ideas flow together smoothly. That means that, if you use them properly, they can work wonders in almost any situation.

And because they're really just plain old everyday words, no-one will suspect that anything out of the ordinary is going on.

Hypnotic Themes Set the Perfect Feeling

We've already touched upon a couple of hypnotic themes. The main principles for a number of hypnotic processes are relaxation and feeling comfortable. They are often called trance themes, but this is just another way to explain the same thing.

Other hypnotic concerns might be comfort, security, harmony, unconsciousness, dreaming, or even hypnosis.

To turn it into a smooth and convincing hypnotic conversation, you take whatever hypnotic theme you want to concentrate on and use power words or linguistic bridges.

Even with these five powerful words, if you want to, you can use it for a very long time. And if you throw in a few metaphors or similes, it's simple to see how even the simplest of tales will transform into a compelling adventure in which you have to participate absolutely.

Heat Things Up With Hot Words

Hot words are emotionally charged words. They are built with power and energy, which gives them the ability to penetrate the unconscious mind.

But contrary to other terms you might use, the hot words do something special. They elicit a strong reaction, an emotional response that can come from only one place-the unconscious mind.

And as soon as you get the response, you can start using it as part of the hypnotic process.

Hot words can be used in a multitude of different ways. Inspiring teachers, leaders, and motivational speakers use these hot words.

They are used ubiquitously by newspapers and tabloids to create sensational news. These words are also used by advertising companies in their promotional campaign to grab your attention.

Hot words are designed to grab your attention, to pull you straight into a story, to get you to react, and to elicit an emotion. As you can see, that's most of the ABS Formula in a nutshell.

For example, here's a typical tabloid headline:

Company boss flees the country with stolen cash

A more conservative newspaper could print the same story less dramatically, with a headline like this:

CEO absconds with company profits

Both headlines say the same story, but the first is more engaging. The words 'flees' and 'stolen' are simple, clear, and emotionally packed.

He'd not just left the country; he'd fled. He not only took the money, but he also robbed it. When you read it, your emotions can't help but be stirred, thinking about the greed of the man, his illegal activity, the employees and suppliers who will never be paid, the situation in which he has left his family, and so on.

Of course, there's a real purpose to everything you have read about so far. And that is the intention of creating a hypnotic experience. To place someone into a hypnotic trance; in other words, you can connect with their unconscious mind. But how do you know if you've achieved it?

How to identify when someone is in a trance

You should be able to tell when someone is in a trance.

You should look out for specific trance signals. You will find some people doing one thing and some people doing another because everyone is different.

But once you learn what the signs are, you can locate and discover the trance signals quickly. And the moment you identify them then it is an indication that the person's unconscious mind is paying attention to your suggestions. Below are a few common trance symptoms to watch out for:

- Relaxation of the face
- Changes in breathing
- Dilation of the pupil
- Relaxation of the eyes as if it were being blurry
- Eyes trying to close
- Lack of movement

Those are all signs that someone is heading into a trance. Yet detecting the signals is only the beginning. If you were in a formal hypnotherapy session you might identify the person with these trance signals. You would say to them, for example, that their breathing has slowed down.

Or that they want to close their eyes, or their eyes might have stopped moving. It produces a feedback loop, which further enhances the cycle of trance.

So, if you were just sitting in a restaurant talking to someone, you would actually confess to yourself that the other person is entering a state of trance (and that everything you do works)

It can be daunting when you start to have this much information presented to all of you at once.

But the trick to practice conversational hypnosis really is to put yourself first in a state of H+ and gain confidence in using power words, stories, and metaphors before it is second- nature.

If you gain the confidence to try things out and see how they work, you'll be well on your way to using your conversational hypnosis in your daily interactions.

And when you've done that, you're going to find your conversations becoming stronger, more successful and more attractive to anyone you meet.

4.7 More on Covert Hypnosis Techniques

Here are some techniques for covert hypnosis to help you achieve the desired results.

Eye Cues

People display different types of body language which all rely on what's in their pattern of thought at that particular moment.

Analyzing their body language gives you a general idea of what that person is thinking about; whether it's a picture, sound or feel. This will enable you to find out that whether they are generating the picture or just trying to remember something.

Eye cues give an insight to the way the people manifest their representational system. It all depends on the directional movement of the eyes.

It may sound simple but in fact, mastering requires a lot of practice and is not always guaranteed for using on everyone.

Sub-modalities

The reactions of people to certain details vary considerably. In order to determine exactly what invokes a positive or negative emotion, sub-modalities take a look at the more intricate details of each thought.

This is an effective technique in covert hypnosis, because you can use a meaning of carefully placed words to evoke a certain reaction (eye signals, body language, voice tone, etc.), and once you know what that response generates, you can use those words to activate the feeling again.

Deception

As a hypnotist, if you want to prevent someone from understanding your true intentions, deception is key. When they catch on, you lost your cover.
You have to phrase recommendations in a very subtle way that will easily trick others. Everyone is susceptible to disinformation, creating a made-up reality.
For instance, if you were told by a trusted friend that he has the phone number for a really hot woman today, you would most likely believe him, even if it is not true. Every single day we fall prey to such fictional facts.
This manipulation technique is used by hypnotists, psychics, mediums and clairvoyants to construct an illusion after winning your friendship and your trust.

Misdirection

Magicians use misdirection to draw the audience's attention away from something else to perform an event they don't want to see. It is used in a conversational context for implicit hypnosis.

For instance, if you try to get someone to undertake an action by discreetly planting a suggestion in their mind, they will be actively aware of what you are trying to achieve.

The trick is that you should try to divert their attention by giving the same suggestion but by using different words in a smart manner. This is especially fruitful if you don't want that person to over-analyze your initial suggestion even if they didn't catch on.

Cold Reading

It is used commonly by psychics, mediums, spiritualists and mentalists to create an impression that they might be aware of reading or have some sort of clear-sighted ability. Cold reading will persuade almost everyone to believe in whatever you say.

It involves making a very vague statement following the person's initial observations. For instance, if your aim is to figure out that whether someone is expressive or shy, you might say: "I feel you're comfortable in sometimes expressing yourself, but sometimes you're reflecting on the past." Now the listener will have multiple responses: "Yes, I'm articulate but I don't reflect" –that means they're more expressive "I tend to reflect a lot" –that means they're shyer.

"Yes, you're right" or "Not really"-these answers aren't very detailed so you need to ask for another general statement.

You can then make more clear comments based on their answers depending on their reaction to your general statement, as you'll now know what kind of persons they are.

Warm Reading

It is based on making generalized statements that could be extended to almost all, much like cold reading, but instead does not require any of that person's thoughts or answers from them.

You take this example of warm reading, for example: "It seems you've grown a lot in the last couple of years. You must have gained a lot of experience that have changed your life perspective, and I can see that you've learned a lot from your past mistakes. "As you can see, that assertion can be attributed to practically everyone, but what makes it true in somebody's mind is that almost everybody thinks they're special in some way.

The technique of warm reading is a good 'ice breaker' and helps you to make clear points from the very beginning before they even speak.

Hot Reading

It is the most powerful form of reading through a large stretch and it'll leave your target person totally amazed.

It's transparent and 100 per cent accurate, but it allows you to have previous knowledge of that person without giving them a hint of this knowledge.

It can be difficult to get this information without that person being aware of it. One approach will be to speak directly to someone who knows the person and discloses personal details about their lives.

The subject would conclude that you have a psychic ability because the mind appears to believe things without any inquiry whatsoever.

Ambiguity

Most power-hungry politicians, dictators, and other political leaders hypnotize the people by using vague speeches is a common way. Many so-called great political leaders are nothing but professional orators. Next time in your region there's an election campaign, I want you to pay attention to the kind of terms that different leaders use to get vote and support from you.

You'll know that the political leaders ' remarks are devoid of logic most of the time. They're full of ambiguities and cryptic slogans that serve no reason other than inciting crowd emotions. A rational leader who uses straightforward, unambiguous speech, and who is not manipulating people's emotions, hardly wins an election.

You must remember that the political leaders' speeches are most of the time devoid of any logic, full of confusion and ambiguous phrases that serve no reason other than to stimulate the crowd's emotions. A rational leader who uses straightforward, unambiguous speech and doesn't stir up people's emotions seldom wins an election.

The important question is: How does ambiguous language finds its way in hypnotizing people? If I tell you simple, logical and meaningful phrases, your conscious mind can have no difficulties in finding out what I'm saying. For example: "Vote for me, because I have prepared a lot of great economic and social policies that will surely improve our country's economic and social conditions.

Boring!

On the other hand, it has a tremendous effect if I use vague words and focus at instigating the emotions. Your conscious mind is busy interpreting my sentence's logical context (which doesn't exist). In the meantime, I am bombarding you with suggestions for voting for me. For instance, "Deceitville people! I ask you to take the challenge RISE UP! I'm demanding that you wake up and welcome Change! We Should, together. This time we're going for peace and growth! We choose the Democratic Party of Hanan this time! "I'm asking you to rise to that challenge? What change is it that I am asking you to embrace?

When your conscious mind is busy seeking answers to these unanswerable questions, I throw in the "suggestion" of voting for me that hits your subconscious mind directly. My chances of winning Deceitville's election are set to increase dramatically.

Conjunctions

The use of conjunctions is both a typical conventional and a covert technique for hypnosis. This covert hypnosis technique involves at first stating a few absolute truths that can be instantly validated by your audience or subject.

After presenting a series of correct information, you give the suggestion that you hope to program your audience's mind or the subject, linking it to the rest of the information through conjunction like' because.'

You can think of your subconscious mind as a club and your conscious mind as the security guard protecting the club. The security guard's job is to ensure that no one enters the club that has the potential to cause some form of danger to the people inside it. Similarly, your conscious mind has to hold away from any knowledge you do not agree with. The guard is alert at first, and carefully frisks every person entering the club. In any conversation, when we begin to scrutinize carefully what the other person is saying, mainly if he is a stranger, we are most conscious in the initial stages.

He becomes less vigilant, exhausted, and lazy when the guard searches several people and doesn't find something suspicious about any of them. He's making tests less severe.

When we continue in a conversation and create confidence, we lower our guard and do not find it appropriate to scrutinize and interpret every word that the other individual expresses.

Around this point, thanks to the security guard's weariness and nonchalance, a criminal is likely to carry a gun into the club without being noticed.

When you've developed trust with a speaker on a conscious or unconscious level, he gains the power to configure your mind with whatever suggestion he likes.

Take a look at this typical speech during an election campaign given by a political leader. Picture yourself as an audience member... "Ladies and gentlemen! As I stand before you on this beautiful and charming occasion tonight, I'm pretty sure you've all gathered here with a lot of enthusiasm and excitation. I sense the same excitement as I feel in addressing you at this point and time. The reason you are here is that you believe in our party and our mission. You don't even have to look around in order to know there are ladies and gentlemen around. While used to get publicity, this statement is registered by your mind as fact.

"When I stand before you tonight..." he's standing in front of you tonight, of course. Another truth and potential are most definitely a lovely and beautiful one too.

"You've all gathered here..." There's no denying that you've all gathered here tonight, and are full of excitement. What a useless expression, to say the least. People who gather to hear somebody speak are usually excited. The intention here is to state an obvious truth, so you can start trusting the speaker.

He throws in his suggestion after building confidence: "You believe in our party and our mission."

Note how the speaker uses the' because' conjunction to connect two entirely unrelated statements. You all gather here on this glorious occasion and have nothing to do with believing in the group or purpose of the speaker.

All of you have come here just to learn what the aim of the party is and then to decide for yourself whether or not to believe it. But because you have developed trust with the speaker, you will probably accept his suggestion that has been followed by a series of absolute truths.

Here's what the' because' conjunction does: your mind searches for a reason to believe this argument when you hear the phrase, "You believe in our party and our goal." You have already been hypnotized at this point. So instead of looking for a rational reason to believe this argument, you accept the illogical explanation pre-provided by the speaker, i.e., "On this wonderful occasion, you've all gathered here."

You are enthralled and hypnotized by the speaker before you know it, and strongly believe in their mission. It doesn't matter; you don't even know what it really is yet.

Presuppositions

Presuppositions are essential since we usually confuse a person's conscious mind at the start of hypnosis. We subsequently add a suggestion. But the opposite is happening in presupposition. First, we make the suggestion and then confuse the person's conscious mind to avoid his scrutiny.

Suppose I am a salesman in an insurance company and trying to sell you a policy. My purpose is to program your mind with the idea, "Our policies are special and effective," which you clearly do not yet believe.

If I just burst out, "Our policies are special and trustworthy," you won't believe it, and your mind will be like, "Oh, really? Why would I think so? Provide me with evidence. Such deliberate examination is what we seek to remove in presuppositions so that the suggestion is considered without any doubt.

So instead, I tell you, "Our policies are not only special and effective, but they also provide long-term protection and benefits for you." Or something like, "We also provide you with all sorts of customer support and 24/7 assistance apart from our special and effective policies."

I confuse your conscious mind by giving it different information to think about by presupposing my idea as an unquestionable truth. And my purpose is not under review.

At this point, you probably won't question my statement that "our policies are specific and effective." Alternatively, you might ask something like, "What kind of protection and benefits will I get in the long term? "Or "What sort of customer service do you offer?"

Analog marking

Analog marking certainly sounds complicated, but in conversations, we all do it naturally. It means emphasizing different keywords and phrases in a conversation. The goal is to communicate directly with the unconscious mind of a person.

The unconscious mind is designed to keep an eye on environmental changes. This is the Oriental Response. When you're in a room, and someone walks in through the door, you turn your head instinctively to see who it is. This may seem like a deliberate answer, but this is not the case most of the time. It's automatic most of the time and happens without your will and involvement.

This behavioral reaction is an integral part of our genetic legacy. It was useful thousands of years ago because people were forced to defend themselves from predators. At that time, the degree of understanding of the environmental changes could have made the difference between life and death.

In short, the subconscious mind automatically perceives every change in the environment. This is the reality we exploit in the marking of analogs. By causing some kind of environmental change when we're transmitting our message during the conversation, we increase the chances of communicating directly with our subject's subconscious.

Analog marking steps

First of all, you need to build confidence and relate to the person you're talking to. This can be achieved by mentioning a few real facts, laughing, looking polite, or using a mirroring technique.

Decide in advance which message you want to send to the unconscious mind of the person. Let's say it is "Let yourself feel comfortable" because it can be beneficial to make sure that a person feels comfortable with you.

Think of a situation where the message you want to send wouldn't be out of place, for example, thinking about a beach visit. "I like to visit the beach where you can just relax and feel comfortable, and look at the waves of the sea." Then speak about the meaning using an expression that can fit the embedded message. "I like to visit the beach where you can just relax and feel comfortable, and look at the sea waves." When you get to the embedded message, "let yourself feel comfortable," do something to mark it out for the unconscious mind of the person to remember. You can do that by lowering your voice tone, relaxing your voice, touching their shoulder, raising your eyebrows, tilting your head, and so on.

The use of the declining voice pitch in analog marking is found to be very successful.

Voice pitch

Vocal pitch is a measure of its shrillness. The shriller the sound, the more it is said to be high-pitched. Only think of it this way to understand it-men generally have low-pitched voices, and women have typically high-pitched voices.

The pitch and tone of your voice decide what sort of a sentence you're saying at a deep unconscious level.

I would like you to do some exercise. I want you to say loudly in three different ways, "What did you do?" Next, tell it with a lifting pitch where your initial voice is flat and soft. Then, near the end, it gets loud and sharp. You will find our mind is interpreting the rising pitch as a query. You ask the other person what he just did out of curiosity. It also refers to arousal.

First, say the phrase with a standard pitch where at the end of the sentence, the voice has the same medium pitch as at the start. The mind processes a flat, pitched voice as a comment. You probably know what the other person did, and your frustration is conveyed.

Finally, tell it with a pitch going down where the voice is at first bright and loud. It then becomes feeble and eventually sluggish towards the end. Our mind interprets a pitched voice that descends as an order. You are probably upset at what the other person did and demand an explanation.

The descending pitch opens somebody's mind to the command module. People are more likely to do what you're telling them to do when you're speaking in a descending pitch because their minds are interpreting it as a command.

Chapter 5: Brainwashing And Covert Persuasion

Brainwashing is the idea that specific psychological methods can change or manipulate the human mind. Brainwashing reduces the ability of its subjects to think critically or autonomously. This allows the introduction into their minds of new, unwelcome thoughts and ideas, which changes their behaviors, values, and beliefs. In 1950 Edward Hunter first used the word "brainwashing" to explain how the Chinese government managed to make people cooperate with them. Studies into the definition have explored and looked into Nazi Germany, several U.S. criminals' cases, and human traffickers ' acts.

In the 1970s, there was much scientific and legal discussion, as well as media attention, about the possibility of brainwashing being a factor in the recruitment of young people into some new religious sects, which at that time were often called the cult. Sometimes the idea of brainwashing is involved in litigation, particularly concerning child custody, and is also a theme in science fiction and in the critique of contemporary political and corporate culture.

Though the word "brainwashing" appears in the fifth edition of the American Psychiatric Association's Diagnostic and Statistical Manual of Mental Disorders (DSM-5), it is generally not recognized as a scientific term.

5.1 Steps and Tricks for Brainwashing

If you want to learn how to brainwash others, just look at any cult, and you'll see the method they use to recruit new members, change their attitude and values, and keep them interested. The same process is used by manipulators in intimate relationships too.

A psychopath's lack of empathy and feelings is typically necessary to be able to control/destroy another person deliberately entirely and in a calculated fashion.

Destruction is what someone calls into brainwashing. It's not just about modifying their ideas, and it's about changing their view of the world, their thought strategies, their emotions, their decision-making, and behaviors. In turn, you are transforming the personality or character of a person into something else. When incorporated, such improvements will last for years unless the victim tries to reverse them intentionally.

So, what is brainwashing?

Let's briefly go through some of the steps involved in brainwashing

- Choose your target
- Give them something they want
- Make them feel unique, desired, valued

- Make their attention conditional, conditional on doing them and thinking about what you want
- Turn to something bigger they want.
- Criticize who they are and start unfreezing their personalities
- Isolate them from everyone and their history so that you become their primary source of knowledge
- Use fear and guilt to make them think differently and make decisions
- Keep them busy physically and mentally so that they have no time to reflect and interrupt normal functions.
- Ensure that they are dependent on you and at the same time scare them by installing leaving phobias
- Make use of rewards and punishments to freeze new ideas, beliefs, and behaviors in place
- Wash, rinse, repeat

It may be appropriate to jump from one step to another or to go back and repeat several steps. Several things may occur at the same time, and so on.

Such phases occur in a cult, in a work situation, in a social situation, and in an intimate relationship, though in each case, they can appear different. A detailed illustration is given below for your understanding.

The Offer

Cults have an external façade used to draw members. It can be personal life, faith, fitness, politics, sports, or the stuff of any kind. Citizens aren't part of a cult. They can join a sales training course to boost or strengthen their ties. Each group has something which they offer to people, and they know it's different for the group; you can't get anything like it from anywhere else, and it promises to fulfill your dreams. Although their target group may seem unique, participants are easily led to believe that the group is going to work for virtually everyone, and they are acting accordingly, trying to bring everyone along.

The' what's on offer' in intimate relationships is a very complex situation. The manipulator assesses their goal efficiently, and works out their interests, wants, wishes, fears, limitations, and even strengths. The manipulator will then give the victim whatever he desires. For instance, this could be anything from a job to a company, to help solve a problem, to a place to stay, and advice, a shoulder to cry on, a relationship with marriage commitment and children. The victim is being cheated about in any situation. Manipulators conceal all kinds of information, they tell lies outright, and they sugar-coat things to make them more appealing.

Love bombing

When the individuals arrive at the group session, they are bombed with love. This means the members of the group make them feel very comfortable, talented, loved, unique, and cared for. It has been found to have a very powerful effect on new people, making them feel part of the group instantly as if they've made instant friends. It makes sharing information about themselves and taking the next step very straightforward for the new victim. It is hard to turn down the offer of more from such friendly people, even if the 'more' isn't exactly what you want.

In intimate relationships, the same operation functions in a subtle way. The victim starts feeling like they've found their dream partner. A new person seems to tick all the boxes of their lives, and the victim feels welcomed, respected, and cherished. The victim opens up to the manipulator and discloses personal details about himself.

This love-bombing is intended to get the victim to agree to further participation in the relationship, be it in a cult or one-to-one situation or a work environment.

The details revealed by the victim will be used later on against them.

Withhold attention

The rules of the group are implemented in a cult while the general focus is on the group theme (health, sales, diet, etc.). Sometimes it's done openly, often clandestinely. The new member finds that doing other things in some way causes the other member to separate themselves, and doing certain things gives more of the very pleasant, positive attention. The newbie quickly learns that they must think and act in some way in order to feel good and remain in the good graces of the leader and the party. In this way the group molds the ideas and actions of the members.

In very close relationships, all that unconditional love at the start of the relationship suddenly becomes conditional. The victim discovers that doing these things upsets the' ideal partner' and they quickly adjust to fix things again. The victim discovers that the actions which were appropriate in the beginning are no more relevant. The manipulator changes the terms and conditions of the partnership such that if the victim wants to be handled kindly they have to change the manipulator's way they relate. For example, when the relationship has been built (so far) on love and happiness and mutual understanding no-one likes being given the silent treatment. The desire to avoid having such pleasant attention being withheld is very high.

Shifting Goals

The new members are led through a process very soon after becoming part of the group, whereby the thing that initially attracted them to the group is converted into a desire for something bigger. The general idea marketed to them is this: "See how good you feel about what we're doing here. Imagine if more people knew about this. How much better would the world be? You'd like to help create such an environment, wouldn't you?" Hence, people who come along for weight loss start taking the goods, and then they get the idea that if they sold products themselves, they could have the profit.

An individual who goes to a seminar to develop their communication skills is led to believe it would be better to start by improving themselves and that doing so would automatically enhance their communication skills. We are led to believe that it is to their overall benefit to turn to constructing the' ideal self.'

The person who is looking for a personal relationship with God is told to go out and spread the word in their own relationship. They are further leveraged into recruiting members by being told, "You wouldn't want to offend God, right now, would you?" A typical tactic of the manipulators in intimate relationships is to do everything about the relationship. "I'm doing this for the sake of the relationship. What are you doing for us? You want this partnership to succeed, don't you? Later, the leader, whether in a cult or intimate relationship, turns his attention to himself. The cult leader clearly states that it is only the victim who can achieve this bigger goal. The members come to believe that nothing has value unless it has to do with the leader. In order to do this, the leader tells stories to boost their own importance, they claim to have exclusive authority and secret knowledge, and they take credit for anything good that happens within 50 yards of them.

Personal Criticism

The cult and manipulators blame and criticize their victims in an intimate relationship, a lot! But this is not just about anything old. They can use any old thing to attack, but the critique is aimed at the individual's personality, at their sense of themselves. Rather than criticize action or opinion or belief, the manipulator explicitly criticizes the individual for a specific behavior or for holding a belief. So instead of' that's a stupid thing to do,' it's' you're stupid (for doing or thinking that).' This is very important, because they have a profound effect on the individual, along with the constant repetition of these remarks. They chip away at self-esteem and start undoing the personality of an individual. A feeling of guilt and shame overwhelms the victim. He feels ashamed of himself tries to mold himself in a way so as to satisfy the manipulator.

Isolation

Manipulators will do many things to separate their victims from family and friends, and from any other network of support, they may have. The reason they do so is that they want to be the primary source of information for the victim. Caring family members will tell the victim they're in a cult or abusive relationship so clearly, the manipulator doesn't want the victim to learn about that. The only way to keep it from happening is either not making contact with others, or not believing or acknowledging what friends and family are telling them.

The manipulators can employ different methods to isolate the victims from their loved ones. For example, convincing members that if they don't help them, their family doesn't love them. Of course, a family does not accept a loved one in a cult, but sometimes when the family knows what's going on, the participant has been inoculated against any backlash that the family may have against the community or the leader. The survivor has thus been conditioned not to pay attention to anything the family says, or even to protect the party vigorously.

If friends do not join the group, the member is told that these non-believers will hold them back and that they should cut them off.

Members are even separated from themselves by strategies such as name changes, rewriting of past history, not being allowed to talk about certain subjects or participate in certain events, having to use a specific language, dress up in a certain way and adopt particular hairstyles or having to change to fit in the lifestyle of the community.

Victims are segregated from strangers but strongly encouraged to spend time with other group members as a way to reinforce group ideas. Members support each other in adhering to the rules and affirm each other's community values. That helps to build the cult's mindset of' us vs. them.'

Leaders of Emotional Control

The cult is never allowed to get angry or frustrated about the leader or the party. Any frustration or anger is diverted at outsiders.

Fear and guilt are the two primary emotions that are used to manipulate people in situations of stress. Fear of the outsiders, fear of community or leader disapproval, fear of losing what has been learned, fear of critical thinking, fear of leaving is some of the more common items that are used to keep people docile and obedient.

In such cases, shame is the other major factor. Victims also don't know how much remorse they feel in the world because the manipulators regularly use this control mechanism. Victims are blamed for anything wrong, while the perpetrator takes credit for everything that goes well. The participants are continually forced to take personal responsibility for all kinds of things. They are placed in a never-ending loop of trying to reinvent themselves to avoid bad things happening so that they can' attain their potential.' This personal responsibility aspect often breaks down people's personalities. Because of the psychological pressure applied to them, more than one person has actually had a nervous breakdown or committed suicide.

The anxiety and remorse is a perfect way to push people to think and make decisions. Individuals are going to make the decisions to escape anxiety and guilt. The leader doesn't always have to tell people what to do in this manner; he only creates anxiety and shame in relation to A so that the members choose B. B, of course, is what the leader wanted first and doing something like this has the benefit for the leader that the members think they make their own choices.

Keep the subject busy

The leader is going to keep the victims occupied. Busy mentally and physically. There are drills to be performed in religion, instruments to be learned, and methods to be studied. There are books, DVDs, audios and so on with plenty of information to absorb. And when you finish them all, you're told it's worth going through them all over again.

And then, there are lists of your wishes, desires, beliefs, goals to test, recheck, rewrite, update, and so on. What's more, the members are expected to tell us, spread the word, educate the world... There is never a dull, slow moment in a cult. There's always something to examine for a deeper meaning to discover... A useful lesson to learn... To get a profound insight. And all that is mental gymnastics. It is of no real value to the leader of the cult, but what it does is to keep them in the cultural mindset.

The manipulators will also keep their victims occupied in intimate relationships, making housework, child care, banking, Bank and Post Office trips. A classic for the manipulators in terms of keeping their victims mentally occupied is to tell a generous person that they are mean or a friendly person that they don't really care about others or an honest person that they are a liar. This often puts the head of the victim in a circle, seeking to find out what the manipulator means. "Why would she say that? Would she see something I don't? Do other people think of me as... when I thought I was the opposite? What do I lack here?" If the group can keep the members so busy that they don't have much time to sleep, all the better!

Fatigued people cannot physically resist. And if the group can get people to eat a diet low in protein, they'll do that too. Then throw in music, dancing, singing, hypnosis, meditation, and you've got people who can't think well anymore but are very vulnerable to suggestion and manipulation in reality.

Cults can push people to be insecure about their own feelings, to think their own ego is their problem. Cults are going to suggest Members should stop thinking and criticizing.

The leaders will very quickly agree the leader is perfect and have all the answers to life's problems. We would embrace fake scientific research dressed up as evidence and will even endorse all kinds of ideas without any evidence at all, without ever challenging them. They entered the realm of blind Obedience at this point.

Dependency

The leaders would make their victims dependent on them. Criticizing the victim for thinking independently and making their own decisions, criticizing their actions, alternating criticism and praise, undermining the identity of the person, and creating phobias of departure are some of the tactics that cults leaders and manipulators use in intimate relationships to establish a childlike dependency in the victims.

Cult members and other victims also come to see themselves as being co-dependent when justifying their sense of dependency on the manipulators. This is a flaw of reasoning since it reverses cause and effect. The victim feels they have a dependent personality, and that's why they ended up with this person who dominates them. The truth is they are dependent because they are with the manipulator. This is actually part of the essence of the cults that were forced upon them.

Refreezing

We have discussed some of the brainwashing techniques that were used to unfreeze the personality of a victim and how different methods are used to get people to think differently, to make different decisions and act differently.

Once these things are in place, once this new world view is in place by the cult member (or partner in an intimate relationship) who behaves and feels according to the wishes of the leader, this new system is refrozen in place, usually using a simple system of rewards and punishments. The individual behaves in compliance with the law and they are rewarded, they break the 'rules' and are punished. This way this new identity is frozen and preserved in the course of time. It becomes the victim's new default.

More information is available on the development of the identity of the cult and the techniques used to construct it.

This cult personality, or fake personality, is obedient to the leader and is faithful to him. If someone criticizes him or her it is conditioned to defend the chief. He is programmed to trust and obey his leader and respect his commands. It's also very leadership-dependent. In reality, the leader becomes the pseudo-personality purpose of life and the pseudo-personality organizes itself around the leader.

The pseudo-personality perception is quite skewed, and it does not understand the leader's influence over it. Nor can it see the group or partnership inconsistencies, such as the fact that the leader does something the members are not allowed to do.

Pseudo-personality views are very strong, often much stronger than normal convictions. Human beings tend to maintain their values intact under normal circumstances, and will sometimes neglect or even reject knowledge that contradicts those beliefs. The intensity of the pseudo-personality assumptions means that ignoring or rejecting knowledge works in cult members and other victims of psychological abuse at an increased level. This is one of the prime reasons that it is very challenging to persuade them they're in an abusive situation.

Repeat

This cycle happens time and time again in religion. The leader actively manipulates and exploits the members to retain the pseudo-personality in place. At the same time the older members bring in new members and put them through the steps (because the fake personality is programmed to attract and indoctrinate new members).

Cults like to have members frequently come to cult activities. It also offers leadership a chance to' top up' the fake identity while taking money from them. Many organizations require participants attend an event every six to twelve months to keep their learning up-to-date with developments from the group. What happens, of course, is that the pseudo-personality is strengthened.

Some organisations make people go back to the beginning of the indoctrination process and go through it again, as a' punishment' for wrongdoings. That serves two purposes at least, the first being punishment and the second being re-indoctrination.

An important thing to remember is that cult methods, resources, procedures, and tactics are all sold as being beneficial to what they are selling, whether its money making, staying well, personal development, faith, or anything else. But, these aspects have been twisted in such a way that they all act to brainwash the people, erase their real personality and substitute it with the cult personality that only thinks and acts for the benefit of the leadership. At the same time, the members believe fully that the leader supports them!

Chanting mantras

This usually is one of the striking features of many religions, especially Buddhism and Hinduism, and almost every church has some kind of hymn-singing worship. As each church member chants or sings the same words, their voices merge into one song, creating a strong sense of oneness and group identity. This, combined with established singing effects such as lowered heart rate and relaxation, could cast the experience of community worship into a positive light. But the repeated repetition of short intonations in cult is intended to create mind-numbing, suppress logical thinking and trigger a state of trance. Increased suggestibility is a characteristic of such a state, and failure to sustain the trance is always accompanied by punishment imposed on cults, ensuring constant implementation of ultra-conformist behaviour.

Psychologists Linda Dubrow-Marshall and Steve Eichel have researched how "being subjected to repetitive and sustained hypnotic inductions can inhibit the ability of the convert to make decisions and interpret new information," adding that "continuous lectures, singing and chanting are used by most cults to alter consciousness."

Active Pedagogy

How does an instructor motivate their students to follow good behavior and conformism? The solution is always to integrate some form of physical activity or sport into their teaching. Absorbed in jumping on the spot or playing around, and therefore exhausted, children are less likely to protest or cause trouble. Recognizing this trend, many cults sought to have members busy as a means of control with endless series of tiring tasks. For example, some suspect cults such as Dahn Yoga are just physical exercise programs on the surface. Mass athletic activities like calisthenics in stadiums in Russia were a familiar characteristic of the Soviet system, and historians equate them with the authoritarian state apparatus. What distinguishes exercise pedagogy from pure sports is that the improved mood and group identity felt during physical activity will be used by a dictatorship or religion to enforce ideological beliefs that might otherwise be met with scepticism.

Exhaustion by exercise is yet another manner in which the barriers of people can be torn down as a means to enable them to embrace dubious ideas.

Sleep Deprivation and Exhaustion

Our ability to make good decisions crumbles by a combination of sensory overload, disorientation and sleep deprivation. Amway, a multi-level marketing corporation, has been charged with depriving its distributors of sleep during weekend-long events, including non-stop seminars lasting until the early morning hours, with only brief interludes during which bands play loud music with flashing lights.

Sometimes used in combination with sleep deprivation, a cult technique involves instructing participants to adopt special diets that include low protein and other important nutrients. As a result, the leaders of the cults will always feel tired, leaving them unable to challenge the demands of religious ideology. On the twentieth anniversary of the Aum Shinrikyo sarin nerve gas attack, the Japan Times interviewed an ex-cult member, who described "eating one meal a day and sleeping a few hours each night" while working on an effort to get the leader of the cult elected to parliament.

Self-criticism and finger-pointing

During the Korean War, American soldiers captured by the Chinese were subjected to sessions of "criticism and self-criticism" in which they had to criticize fellow prisoners, address their own shortcomings and demonstrate their insecurities regarding capitalism and the United States. The POWs at first felt the sessions were infantile. Yet over time, the continuing vital process began to cause them to manifest real doubts about their patriotism and the war's validity.

Psychologist Robert Cialdini would describe the prisoners ' the anxiety as a result of the "law of commitment," which means that we are trying to keep our thoughts in line with our public statements, since we don't like being inconsistent or deceptive.

With some small achievements, overall, the methods of "brainwashing" in the Korean War have not been particularly effective. At the end of the war, only 23 POWs declined repatriation and the Chinese had already given up the reeducation sessions a year before the war ended. Yet domestically they tended to use similar practices.

Mystical Manipulation

Psychiatrist Robert Jay Lifton claims that many cults rely on "mystical manipulation" to gain complete control over their followers. Mystical deception refers to the regulation by cult leaders of situations or knowledge to give the illusion that they are controlling spiritual intelligence, divine favor or magical powers. In other words, supposed religious leaders are presenting themselves as the infallible messenger of God, whose judgment must always be true and correct, and are endorsing this through dazzling tricks and incredible gimmicks.

George Roden, one of David Koresh's early rivals for Branch Davidians leadership, theatrically exhumed a corpse that he vowed to return to life to prove his necromantic abilities. His rival was challenged to do the same, but instead Koresh actually reported him to the police for the grave robbery. The police asked Koresh for evidence and a gunfight erupted as

Koresh's group attempted to gain access to the compound where Roden kept the corpse.

In truth, Koresh himself was known at the time as Vernon Howell, but later changed his name to indicate descent from the biblical King David. Following Cyrus, the Great, a Persian king who liberated the Jews from Babylonian Captivity, he adopted the last name Koresh. Koresh developed a messianic persona and allowed his followers to attribute to divine intervention extraordinary events when he had personally orchestrated them.

Barratry Violence

Most cults hire lawyers to sue anyone who criticizes them publicly, no matter how trivial the criticism. Of course, a cult can typically afford to lose the cases, while ex-cult leaders are often insolvent after giving their life to the organization. Consequently, many ex-cultists are unable to mount an effective legal counterattack.

However, due to the ever-present threat of legal action, mainstream journalists are afraid to condemn cult or reference religious material. In 2003, Rick

Ross, a prosecutor, collected excerpts from NXIVM's books, a self-improvement group suspected of cultic practices. Ross put the extracts online, only to be met with litigation and rifling inquiries into his garbage. Several NXIVM workers who left the organization have faced substantial legal proceedings. A judge dismissed one of those lawsuits, recognizing that the employee in question had merely attempted to leave, only to be "labeled as' suppressive,' a concept that NXIVM extends to former associates leaving the company or whom NXIVM perceives to be its rivals, and subjected to protracted litigation by two major law firms and a phalanx of lawyers." In 1967, Ron Hubbard wrote that "we do not consider Scientology critics who have no criminal past" and that litigation should be used to censor such potentially culpable critics. "The object of the[lawsuit] is to threaten and intimidate rather than win." Well aware of the implications of offending Scientologists, HBO recruited 160 lawyers preemptively to defend their 2015 Going Clear series. Deterred from striking back in the courts, the church launched a "brutal" campaign against people who appeared in Alex Gibney, the film director.

Thought Terminating Cliches

Another essential concept proposed by Robert Jay Lifton is the notion that totalitarian regimes frequently rely on "thought-finishing clichés" to impose obedience on their subjects. Through these clichés, "the most far-reaching and complex of human problems are distilled into short, highly reductive, definitive words." The classic example of Lifton was the "all-encompassing jargon" of Communist regimes such as China and the Soviet Union, where the language was "abstract, extremely categorical, and essentially" the language of non-thought. Modern non-state organizations such as the Church of Scientology may have developed a series of phrases roughly equivalent to Soviet jargon.

Perhaps the most prominent example of 'thought-terminating clichés' comes from Nazi official Adolf Eichmann's trial. The writer Hannah Arendt noted in her famous book on Eichmann and the "banality of evil" that the SS leader often spoke in stock phrases and clichés. Eichmann reiterated that he wished to "make peace with his former enemies." Still, Arendt concluded that the expression was meaningless because he did not understand the extent of his crimes at all — only in the vocabulary of National Socialism could he think of those. Arendt argued that the wartime "German culture of eighty million people was protected by precisely the same means, the same self-deception, lies, and ignorance toward truth and factuality."

5.2 Covert Persuasion Techniques

These are some of the most effective methods of selling and encouragement you will ever learn. By using them, you can place an idea into a person's mind -such as the urge to purchase your product or sign up for your MLM Company -while persuading them that it was their idea rather than yours.

There are some powerful methods of persuasion which are used by most successful people and prominent companies. Such methods of persuasion operate on the subconscious, and if properly understood and applied, will produce top-notch results. We also studied the best techniques which are mostly focused on the influence of Robert Caldini.

Using Covert Persuasion Techniques in Selling or Marketing

Say you are trying to sell a specific product or service using Deceptive Manipulation methods in sales or marketing. Instead of starting with a sales pitch for your company, you are engaging your prospect in a conversation about what they need.

You can begin by telling them that you had the same problem. Once you know what their need is, then tell them how you solved it using the product you are selling.

Here's an important thing to remember when using hidden persuasion tactics: Do not focus on the product's merits, but on how the product can better meet the needs of the prospect or solve the problem. Be honest as you tell them how this product has benefited you. And even if they aren't sensitive yet, never contradict or tell them that they are incorrect.

Using Covert Persuasion Strategies in Motivating People

To motivate people, begin by introducing the target to be reached and the timeline in which it must be accomplished, and then plant a seed of motivation in the mind of the person.

For example, you can tell them, "I know you're a good worker who can complete this job in a week." In doing so, you're putting the idea in their minds that they can reach the target in the given time limit.

Keep in mind that the essence of effective covert persuasion tactics lies in the illusion that you are not actively selling to them or forcing them to do a specific task, but engaging them in a dialogue in which what you are asking them to do it for their own benefit, rather than yours; and most importantly, that it was their own idea.

Foot in the Door Principle

Foot in the door principle means you will ask for a smaller one before asking for a tremendous favor. You're having the person "committed" to support you by first asking for something little, and the more significant request functions as a continuation of something already theoretically agreed upon.

Real-life Application

Ask a visitor for directions. We suggest we can get lost as a follow-up and ask you to walk them there. You are more likely to agree to that than to ask the second question straight-off.

You skipped a class and demanded their notes from your classmates. You eventually admit that you were a tad reckless this semester and ask for the notes for the semester as a whole. Thus, you enhance the probability of getting the big one by first asking for the small favor-namely, a free-ride on the notes of your classmate.

You just missed a significant midterm, and the instructor is not offering retakes. You decide to ask your work for input and why you have struggled, followed by a call for a retake. In such a situation, you're more likely to succeed, as opposed to merely demanding a retake.

Case Study

Two Stanford scholars-Jonathan Freedman and Scott Fraser-decided in 1966 to test the efficacy of FITD as a tool of persuasion. Then 156 women were split into four classes. They called the first three parties, asking some simple questions about their kitchen items for the home.

Three days later, they asked to go through their kitchen cabinet directly, and list their things. With the second request, only the other party was addressed. The first three groups had a compliance rate of 52.8%, while the last group only had 22.2%.

Door in the Face

Hey, would you mind running naked around the streets shouting how amazing this article is? Doesn't it? Ok, could you at least share this on Facebook with your friends?

The door in the face is the reverse of the persuasion strategy referred to above. Here, you are asking for something big they won't agree with, then you are asking for something that is contrastingly simpler.

Real-life application

- In Advanced Statistics, you ask a classmate to mentor you on the upcoming midterm. Oh, and until now, you've not trained at all. The classmate apologizes and says they just don't have the time. Your request to follow up on their notes is granted, however.
- Ask your buddy for a 100$ loan. You question after the "No": "Can I have at least 20?"
- A store has a policy of calling for charitable donations before asking the customer to pay. Some people wouldn't make a donation, but if the cashier asks them to make a donation of $100 and then asks "how about 5," $the number of donations would increase exponentially.

Case Study

A study showed how the DITF methodology could help with retail sales. A saleswoman had been selling cheese to people in the Austrian Alps walking past a shelter. In the first example, a pound of cheese was sold for 4 Euros to the hikers.

In the second scenario, the saleswomen first offered 2 pounds of cheese for 8 Euros and then pleaded for a pound for four after being refused. Compliance rates differ markedly: 9 percent for the first submission, 24 percent for the second request.

Principle of Anchoring

It is a cognitive bias present in most decisions. How do you know, for example, which product is "good?" You equate it to a similar product, and from there make a decision.

There are many different uses to this method; one of the most widely used is pricing. Anchoring can be a useful persuasion tool if used properly.

Real-life Application

You're searching for a new car to purchase and consider a $10,000 OK deal. You negotiate with the seller and manage to reduce the cost to $7,000. You go home contented, talking about how much of a bargain it was. However, the actual value of the vehicle was less than $7,000. The original $10,000 price serves as an anchor, so you'll consider something cheaper than the anchor price as a "good deal."

You've just got a new job offer, with an additional $2,000 a month bid. You are negotiating it to $2,200. Once again, you can get low-balled, as with the previous example. While it may seem appealing to raise by 10 percent over the initial offer, it may still be smaller than the actual value.

Case Study

The Economist used to have three different options to subscribe to.

A) Print online for $59 B) Print $125 and C) Print & Web $125.

16 chose option A, and 84 chose option C on a study done on 100 MIT graduates.

The experimenter then eliminated option B and gave an additional 100 students the same test. In this scenario, 68 selected option A, and 32 selected option C.

The message here is, people are using option B as an anchor. In fact, nobody would choose it; instead it was used only to increase the value of option C.

Principle of Commitment & Consistency

People are susceptible to being consistent with their behavior and beliefs. If you are committing a person to something small, you might use the initial commitment to motivate them to do more for you.

Real-life application

You buy the same brands over and over, most of the time. When was your last attempt on a new snack or drink?

"You can do me a favor? "Sure." "Can you get me a shop beer? "Unlike, "Hey, will you, etc."

You've already learned how setting goals can be helpful in attainment of success. The definition is something rarely left out of a book on self-help. The reason this is successful is because of consistency: you are more mindful that when you have written it down, this is what you want, and should aim for.

Let's presume you're working at an NGO, and collecting money for some reason. You may ask the person before asking for donations if they support the cause. If this is the only the purpose, they will most likely respond positively. You are more likely to earn donations by posing a question like this in the second phase.

Case Study

Many websites that sell a product these days use the concept of quality to get you to sign up for their mailing list. Typically, their pop-ups read something in the lines of, "Yes, sign me up. I love free cash! "And' No, I would slightly have disappointed.'" It helps boost conversion rates.

Social Proof Principle

This article is selected for reasoning-based advice by most of your peers. You, too, should. "Everybody believes this, so it has to be real." Social evidence is one of the most popular methods of persuasion. It does not take long to note that there is a high degree of group-thinking in most social groups. Someone suggests an idea, and everyone just goes along with it–even if everyone disagrees. People are looking at what their colleagues do when making a decision and prefer behaving in a similar fashion.

Real-life Application

If you have an empty tip jar at work, you may be considering filling it up a little before the shift starts. Customers are more likely to tip if they see a full tip jar rather than an empty one —other people's tips, so I should probably do the same

There exists a greater possibility for you to like a Face book post if it already has lots of likes, as opposed to a zero-likes post.

The reason most people take up smoking is because of social proof. Everyone smokes, so you can smoke too —given all the safety issues and awful taste that comes with it.

Case Study

An experiment was performed in 1935. Several subjects were put in a dark room 15 feet away with a dot of light. Instead, the subjects were asked to guess how much the dot traveled. All attendees gave different numbers.

They were put together on the second day and asked the same question. They ended up agreeing on a whole different number this time, far from their previous estimates.

Principle of authority

Persuasion experts believe this article is the best source of persuasion-related advice. In any sector or subject, people look up to authority, so making yourself seem like a source of authority will take you a long way.

Real-life Application

- Many startups or smaller firms placed an "as seen on" logo on their landing pages if they were featured on major media websites. For example, if a business was on Techcrunch, it means fantastic because Techcrunch doesn't just cover everyone.
- Product X won the best iOS app for 2015

- 9/10 dentists agree a specific toothpaste brand is the best one out there. It also gives third world countries clean drinking water. And cancer treatments.
- Companies appear to have their previous clients listed on their landing page. This is particularly valid if they interacted with significant corporations

Case Study

Stanley Milgram, a Yale University psychologist, performed a series of psychological experiments that later became known as the Milgram Experiment. The experiment had three roles— the experimenter, the instructor, and the subject. The instructor, who will be the volunteer, will ask questions from the learner.

The teacher would administer an electric shock if the learner responded correctly. And after the learner was "crying out in pain," the experimenter kept pressuring the teacher to use the electric shock. In most cases, the teacher would only go along with the orders of the experimenter, despite realizing he was causing unnecessary agony to another human being. Eight out of ten teachers managed to deliver the shocks even after their student had stopped hearing any response and thought he had passed away. The lesson here is that most people are willing to obey someone with authority, even when they act on something that is clearly wrong.

Scarcity Principle

This post will expire in the next 5 seconds unless you share it on Face book. Scarcity is one of the most widely used methods of persuasion used by salesmen and marketers. People tend to want more of the low-supply material. When you persuade a person that something is available only for a limited time, or is in limited supply, they're more likely to go for it.

Real-life Application

- Booking.com never fails to point out how only 2-3 rooms are left in that hotel, or how 20 other people look at the same hotel too.
- Some LIMITED TIME ONLY Deal GOING TO CHANGE YOUR LIFE BUY IT NOW.

- Online marketers leverage scarcity by selling their goods once a year for a specific period while stressing how the product provides a limited time chance. Similarly, give a discount, but add a timer, or date of validity, to it. The higher the sales rate, the more you insist on how scarce the commodity is.

- Let's assume you're a door to door salesman. With this technique of persuasion, you can pretty much go wild. For example, you might say you're only for the day in the area, or you're doing a rare, never-to-be-seen-again promo. That is to say, and the consumer will not be able to buy the product at any later date

Case Study

A study was conducted in which 180 students were split into classes. One was presented with a commodity that was supposed to be scarce and the other with a product that was supposed to be abundant. The experiment concluded that it was uncommon for the students to choose the product that was in abundance.

Principle of reciprocation

People like to reciprocate favors and gifts. No matter if the person likes the gift, they are still inclined to give something in return. It's something that will always be beneficial to make others feel indebted to you, increasing the chances of getting what you want exponentially.

Application in real life

Let's say you collect money to help orphans find a new home. You could make a small event before searching for potential donors, where the kids make bracelets from different materials. You might give away the bracelet before asking for a donation, thereby making the potential donor feel indebted.

If I had asked you, in the introduction, to share this article, you would probably not.

Case Study

A study at an expensive New York restaurant found that the more hospitality the waiter showed, the higher the clients would tip. In the first example, the waiter will give each customer a piece of chocolate, resulting in a higher tip of 18 percent.

In the second, the water will start walking away after giving away a piece of candy, turn around, and give another piece of candy of customer's choice. This approach increased the tip amount by 21 percent.

Conclusion

Psychological abuse may be characterized as exercising undue influence through mental coercion and emotional exploitation, with the intention of seizing power, control, benefits and/or privileges at the expense of the victim.

Healthy social control should be differentiated from psychological manipulation. Healthy social impact exists among most individuals, and is part of positive partnership built on giving and taking. However, dark psychology comes into play when one individual is used in psychological manipulation to the advantage of another. The manipulator intentionally creates a power imbalance, and uses the victim to fulfill his agenda.

Given below is a brief overview of some of the important tricks that can be used by covert manipulators to achieve their goals.

It is not necessary that everyone who acts in the following ways can attempt to manipulate you intentionally. Many people have only really bad habits. Regardless, in circumstances where your rights, interests and health are at stake it is important to recognize these behaviors.

Home Court Advantage A manipulative person can demand that you meet and communicate in a physical space where he or she can exert greater control and dominance. This can be the workplace, house, vehicle, or other spaces of the manipulator in which he feels possession and comfort (and where you neglect them).

Let You Talk First to Establish Your Baseline and Check for Weaknesses As they prospect you, many sales people do so. They build a baseline on your thinking and behavior by asking you general and inquiring questions, from which they can then determine your strengths and weaknesses. This form of hidden agenda of questioning can also occur on the workplace or in personal relations.

Distortion of Facts(Deception) Excuse me for making it. Met with two. The blame is put on victim for causing their own victimization. Truth-deformation is at its peak. Dissemination or withholding of key information is done to keep you in dark. Overstatement and understatement is rampant.

Overwhelm You with Facts and Statistics Many people enjoy "intellectual bullying" by presuming to be the most experienced and expert in certain fields. They take advantage of you by forcing on you supposed evidence, figures and other details about which you may know nothing. In sales and financial circumstances, in professional meetings and agreements, as well as in social and personal disputes this can happen. The manipulator hopes to drive forward her or his agenda more convincingly, by presuming expert control over you. For no other motive do some people use this strategy than to feel a sense of intellectual superiority.

Overwhelm You with Regulations and Red Tape Many people use bureaucracy–paperwork, regulations, rules and by-laws, committees, and other roadblocks to maintain their position and control, while making other lives harder. This method can also be used to postpone the discovery of evidence and the search for truth, mask flaws and shortcomings and avoid scrutiny.

Raising Their Voice and Showing Negative Emotions Many people raise their voices as a means of violent provocation during discussions. The presumption may be that you will succumb to their manipulation and give them what they want if they expressed their voice forcefully enough, or show negative emotions. To maximize effect, the aggressive voice is often paired with a strong body language such as standing or excited movements.

Bad Surprises Some people use bad surprises to obtain a psychological advantage and throw you off balance. In a negotiation environment this can range from low balling to a sudden task that she or he will not be able to come through and deliver in some way. Usually, without warning comes the unwelcome negative information, so you have little time to prepare and combat their advance. The manipulator can request more concessions from you to continue working with you.

Giving You Little to No Time to Decide It is a typical sales and bargaining technique where the manipulator puts pressure on you until you are able to make a decision. By adding stress and pressure on you, you are expected to "crack" and to cede to the demands of the aggressor.

Negative humor It is designed to dig at your vulnerabilities and meant to disempower you. Many manipulators like to make critical comments, often disguised as satire or sarcasm, to make you look inferior and less comfortable. These can include any number of remarks ranging from your appearance, to your older smart phone model, history and qualifications, to the fact that you walked slow and got out of breath in two minutes. The aggressor aims to exert psychological dominance on you by making you look bad, and getting you to feel bad.

Judgmental Consistently judge and blame you for making you feel inferior different from the previous conduct in which derogatory humor is used as a cover, here the manipulator chooses you outright. She or he holds you off-balance and preserves her supremacy by continually marginalizing, ridiculing and throwing you off. The aggressor intentionally promotes the illusion that something is always wrong with you, and that no matter how hard you try, you are incompetent and never will be good enough. The manipulator focuses heavily on the negatives without providing concrete and positive ideas or finding practical ways to help.

The Silent Treatment By purposely failing to respond to your rational calls, text messages, emails, or other questions, the manipulator presumes control by making you wait, and aims to inject doubt and uncertainty into your mind. The silent treatment is a game in which silence is used as leverage.

Pretend Ignorance The classic tactic of "playing stupid" is employed by the manipulator. The manipulator / passive-aggressive makes you take on what is her duty by pretending that she or he doesn't understand what you want, or what you want her to do, and gets you to break a sweat... Some kids use this strategy to delay, stall, and trick adults into doing something they don't want to do for them. This technique is also used by some grown-ups when they have something to conceal or a responsibility they want to escape.

Guilt-Baiting Unreasonable Blaming is at the heart of this evil technique. Targeting a soft spot of the victim is the key to success for the manipulator.

By exploiting the emotional vulnerabilities and insecurity of the receiver, the manipulator coerces the receiver into ceding to unreasonable demands and requests.

Victimhood Social problems are presented in a distorted or imagined manner. The health problems are misunderstood or perceived. Dependencies are ubiquitous.

The objective of manipulative victimhood is often to manipulate the good will of the recipient, the culpable conscience, the sense of duty, or the protective and nurturing instinct to obtain unfair benefits and concessions.

References

1. ^ *"Definition of 'Manipulate'"*. *www.merriam-webster.com. Retrieved 2019-02-24.*

2. Jump up to:[a] [b] [c] [d] *Simon, George K (1996). In Sheep's Clothing: Understanding and Dealing with Manipulative People.ISBN 978-1-935166-30-6.* (reference for the entire section)

3. Jump up to:[a] [b] [c] *Braiker, Harriet B. (2004). Who's Pulling Your Strings ? How to Break The Cycle of Manipulation.ISBN 978-0-07-144672-3.*

4. *Kantor, Martin (2006). The Psychopathology of Everyday Life: How Antisocial Personality Disorder Affects All of Us.ISBN 978-0-275-98798-5.*

5. *Skeem, J. L.; Polaschek, D. L. L.; Patrick, C. J.; Lilienfeld, S. O. (2011). "Psychopathic Personality: Bridging the Gap Between Scientific Evidence and Public Policy".Psychological Science in the Public Interest. 12 (3): 95–162.doi:10.1177/1529100611426706. PMID 26167886.*

6. *Frank, Prabbal (2007). People Manipulation: A Positive Approach (2 ed.). New Delhi: Sterling Publishers Pvt. Ltd (published 2009). pp. 3–7. ISBN 978-81-207-4352-6. Retrieved 2019-11-09.*

7. Faggioni M & White M Organizational Psychopaths – Who Are They and How to Protect Your Organization from Them (2009)

8. Baibak, P; Hare, R. D Snakes in Suits: When Psychopaths Go to Work (2007).

9. Jump up to:[a][b][c] *Kernberg, O (1975). Borderline Conditions and Pathological Narcissism. New York: Jason Aronson.ISBN 978-0-87668-205-0.*

10. Jump up to:[a][b] *Aguirre, Blaise (2016). "Borderline Personality Disorder: From Stigma to Compassionate Care". Stigma and Prejudice. Current Clinical Psychiatry. Humana Press, Cham. pp. 133–143. doi:10.1007/978-3-319-27580-2_8.ISBN 9783319275789.*

11. *Baron-Cohen, S (2012). The Science of Evil: On Empathy and the Origins of Cruelty. Basic Books. pp. 45–98.ISBN 978-0-465-03142-9.*

12.   Casillas, A.; Clark, L.A.k (October 2002). "Dependency, impulsivity, and self-harm: traits hypothesized to underlie the association between cluster B personality and substance use disorders". Journal of Personality Disorders. **16** (5):   424–36.doi:10.1521/pedi.16.5.424.22124. PMID 12 489309.

13.   Kernberg, O. (1993). Severe Personality Disorders: Psychotherapeutic Strategies (New ed.). Yale University Press. pp. 15–18. ISBN 978-0-300-05349-4.

14.   ^ "On Manipulation with the Borderline Personality".ToddlerTime   Network. Retrieved 28 December 2014.

15.   ^ American Psychiatric Association 2000

16.   ^ "Histrionic Personality Disorder". The Cleveland Clinic. Retrieved 23 November 2011.

CPSIA information can be obtained
at www.ICGtesting.com
Printed in the USA
LVHW020310230121
677172LV00011B/752